Oxford First Grammar, Punctuation and Spelling Dictionary

OXFORD
UNIVERSITY PRESS

Contents

Introduction

This dictionary will support children aged 5-7 years who are learning about **grammar**, **punctuation** and **spelling** at school. The book has been written and designed for children to look at on their own or with a parent or teacher, with helpful prompts and questions from the bird characters throughout. The answers to the birds' questions can be found at the back of the book.

There is a section on grammar which gives clear meanings for the key words that children need to know, supported by age-appropriate examples. The punctuation section shows the punctuation marks in context and the spelling section provides rules and examples of tricky words.

At the back of the book is a spelling dictionary of key curriculum and frequently misspelt words using analysis of the Oxford Children's Corpus. This is a large database of children's writing that can be analysed for common spelling errors. The words that 5-7 year olds often struggle with are included in the dictionary, along with a simple meaning.

The **appendix** for teachers and parents is provided as a quick reference to see what grammar terms and topics are taught in Y1 and Y2.

The clear headings and full **index** at the back will help users to find the page or section that they need quickly and easily.

The publishers would like to thank the primary teachers and schools, the education consultants and grammarians whose advice and expertise proved invaluable in the compilation of this book.

Grammar

Letter

There are 26 **letters** in the English language.

We use these letters to write down the sounds that we say when we are speaking.

Challenge!

These 26 letters are called the **alphabet**.

Here are the 26 letters:

a	b	c	d	e	f	g
h	i	j	k	l	m	n
o	p	q	r	s	t	u
v	w	x	y	z		

Capital letter

Each letter can also be written as a **capital letter**.

A	B	C	D	E	F	G
H	I	J	K	L	M	N
O	P	Q	R	S	T	U
V	W	X	Y	Z		

We use a capital letter:
- ★ to start a sentence
- ★ for the word '**I**'
- ★ for the names of people, places and days of the week.

Challenge!

Nouns that start with a capital letter because they are names are called **proper nouns**.

See page 12 to find out what a noun is.

Word

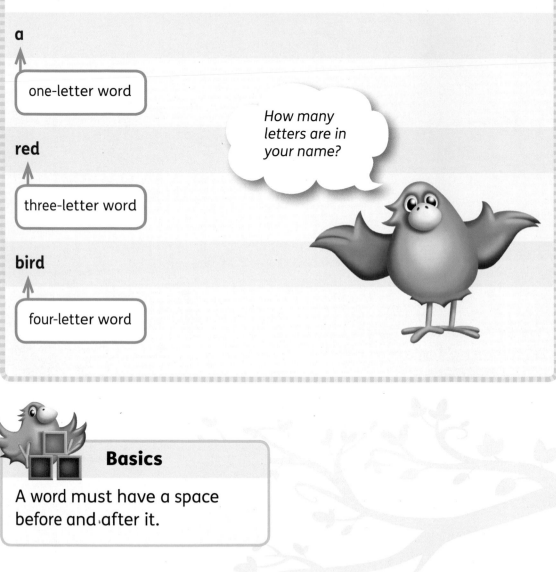

A **word** is made up of one or more letters.

a

one-letter word

red

three-letter word

bird

four-letter word

How many letters are in your name?

Basics

A word must have a space before and after it.

Word class

Different types of words can do different jobs in a sentence. We say they belong to different **word classes**.

Adjectives, **nouns** and **verbs** are all different word classes.

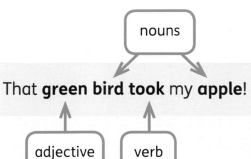

nouns

That **green bird took** my **apple**!

adjective   verb

Challenge!

Some words can belong to more than one word class.
You have to look carefully at the job the word does in the sentence to decide its word class.

The **walk** was long and muddy.

'Walk' is a **noun** in this sentence.

I **walk** to school every day.

'Walk' is a **verb** in this sentence.

Noun

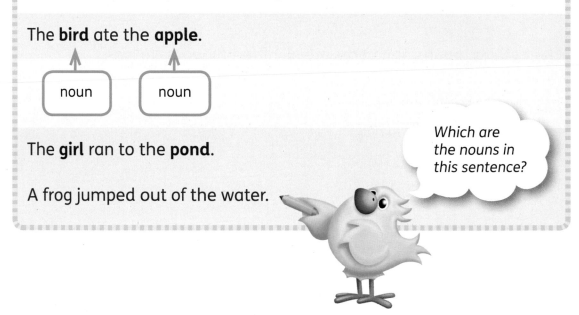

A **noun** names a person or thing. It can be used after **the** or **a**.

The **bird** ate the **apple**.

noun   noun

The **girl** ran to the **pond**.

A frog jumped out of the water.

Which are the nouns in this sentence?

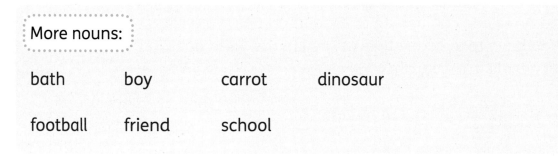

More nouns:

bath   boy   carrot   dinosaur

football   friend   school

Noun

A noun is **singular** if there is just one.

one **bird**

A noun is **plural** if there is more than one.

three **birds**

To make most nouns **plural**, we add an **-s**.

apple + s = apple**s**

If the plural sounds like 'iz', we add **-es**.

box + es = box**es**

If a noun ends in a consonant and **-y**, we change the **-y** into **-i** and add **-es**.

baby → bab**ies**
family → famil**ies**
body → bod**ies**

See page 47 to find out what a consonant is.

Watch out!

A few nouns are the same in the singular and plural.
sheep
deer
fish

Watch out!

A few nouns don't add **-s** or **-es** to become plural, but change in a different way.
man → men
child → children

A **common noun** names people, things and places in general.

cake   car   chair   dog   park   elephant   mat   tree

A **proper noun** names a particular person, place or thing.
A proper noun begins with a **capital letter**.

See page 9 for more about capital letters.

Jack   London   England

The names of **days** are proper nouns.

Monday   Tuesday   Wednesday   Thursday
Friday   Saturday   Sunday

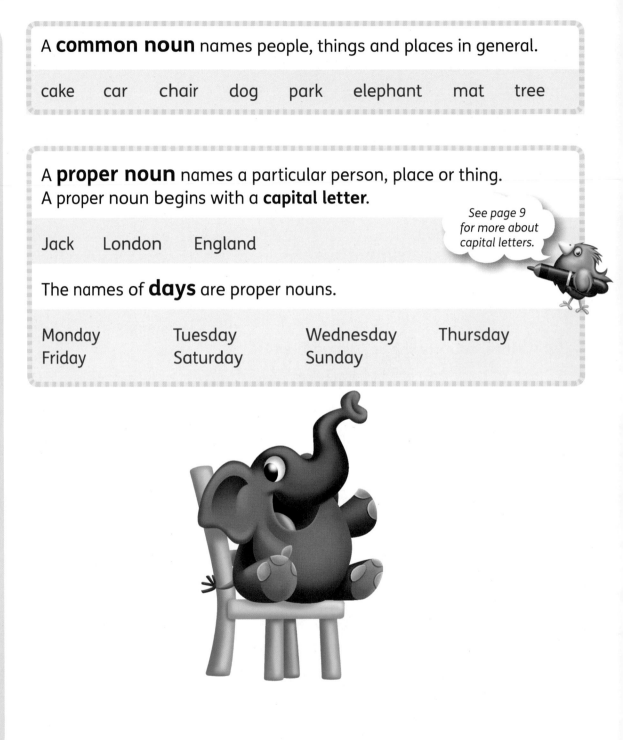

Proper noun

Challenge!

The names of **months** are proper nouns.

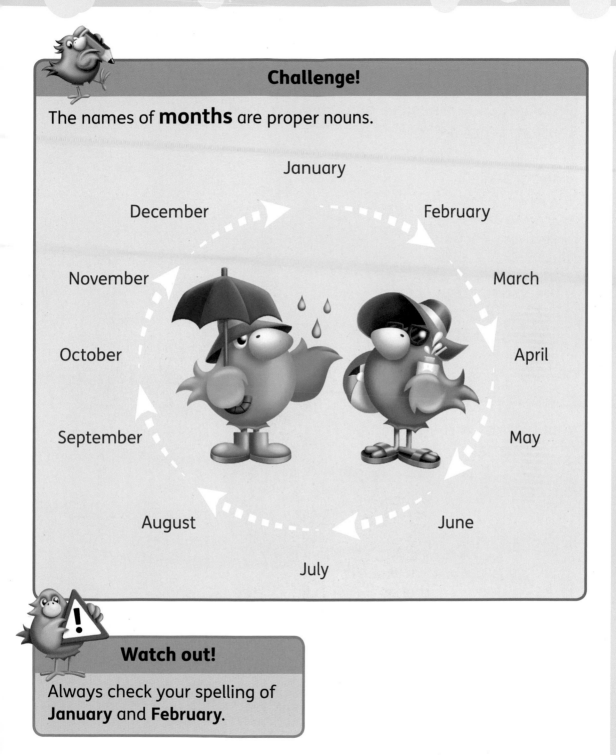

January

December   February

November   March

October   April

September   May

August   June

July

Watch out!

Always check your spelling of **January** and **February**.

Adjective

An **adjective** can tell us more about a noun.
It often comes before a noun.

a **sharp** pencil

| adjective | noun |

a **green** and **purple** pencil

Which are the adjectives in this phrase?

that big, fast car

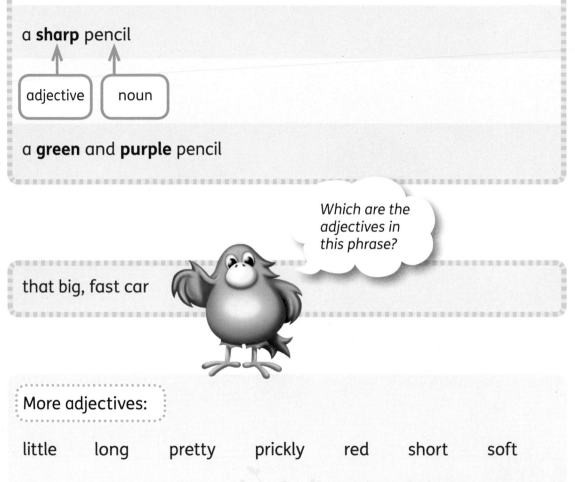

More adjectives:

little   long   pretty   prickly   red   short   soft

An adjective can come after the verbs **is**, **am**, **are**, **was** or **were**.

> The verb forms 'I am, he is, they are' can all come in front of an adjective.

> 'I was, he was, they were' can too.

This egg is **huge**.

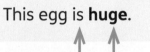

verb   adjective

This egg is **tiny**.

These eggs are **warm**.

More adjectives:

clean   cold   dirty   hot   loud   quiet

Verb

A **verb** is often called a 'doing word'.
It can tell us what someone or something is doing.

The bird **flies** to the tree.

verb

The bird **eats** a worm.

It **sits** in the nest.

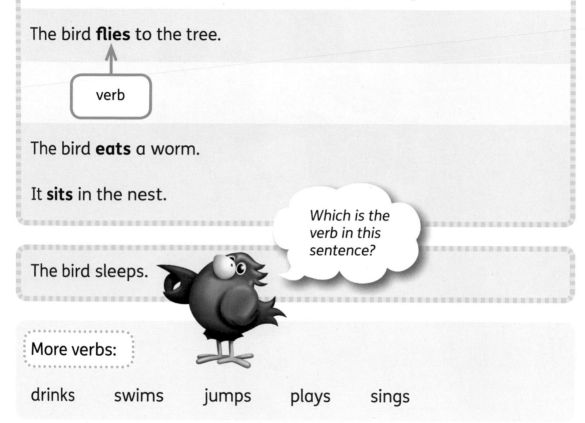

Which is the verb in this sentence?

The bird sleeps.

More verbs:

drinks   swims   jumps   plays   sings

A verb can also be a 'being word'.
It often comes before an adjective.

The bird **is** happy.

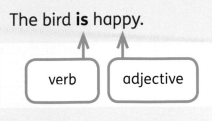

verb adjective

The chicks **are** hungry.

I **am** sleepy.

More verbs:

feels   looks   seems

If you can make a word into a past tense, it is a verb.

The bird **pecks** the apple. (present tense)
↓
The bird **pecked** the apple. (past tense)

I **am** happy. (present tense)
↓
I **was** happy. (past tense)

See page 28 for more about verb tenses.

19

Adverb

An **adverb** can tell us more about a verb.
It can tell us how something is done.

The bird ate the apple **noisily**.

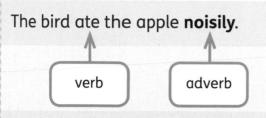

verb   adverb

The cat ran **quickly** up the tree.

Which is the adverb in this sentence?

The bird looked sadly at the empty nest.

More adverbs:

eagerly   happily   loudly   quietly   shyly   slowly

Watch out!

Many adverbs end in **-ly**, but
not all of them.

Adverb

Grammar

Challenge!

An adverb can also tell us when or how often something happens.

Granny is coming **later**.

adverb

My brother **always** plays football on Saturdays.

More adverbs:

soon   then   next   never   recently

Challenge!

An adverb can also tell us more about an adjective or another adverb.

The sun is **terribly** hot.   He ran **really quickly**.

adverb adjective   adverb adverb

More adverbs:

so   very   too   hardly   quite

21

Sentence

A **sentence** is a group of words that make sense on their own.

Here is a bird.

All sentences start with a **capital letter**.

All sentences have a **verb**.

All sentences end with a **full stop**, a **question mark** or an **exclamation mark**.

Challenge!

All sentences have at least one **clause**. A clause is a group of words that make sense together, with a verb as its key word.

Some sentences are made up of just one clause.
These are called **single-clause sentences**.

This bird has some seeds.

Some sentences are made up of more than one clause.
These are called **multi-clause sentences**.

This bird has some seeds and **it is hungry**.

first clause

second clause

There are four types of sentence:
* statements
* questions
* commands
* exclamations.

I love seeds.

A **statement** tells you something. It ends with a full stop.

SEEDS

Can I eat these seeds?

SEEDS

A **question** asks you something. It ends with a question mark.

Take these seeds away.

A **command** tells you to do something. It can end with a full stop or sometimes an exclamation mark.

What delicious seeds these are!

An **exclamation** shows surprise, a cry or strong feeling about something. It ends with an exclamation mark. An exclamation often starts with the words 'what' or 'how'.

See pages 40-41 for more about full stops, question marks and exclamation marks.

Conjunction

Conjunctions link words or groups of words in a sentence. They are sometimes called joining words.

Examples of conjunctions:

and   but   or

I have a sandwich **and** an apple.

conjunction

Would you like a cake **or** a biscuit?

I ate the cake **but** I left the sandwich.

Challenge!

Conjunctions that link words or groups of words that are equally important are called **co-ordinating conjunctions**.

I like cats **and** I love dogs.

co-ordinating conjunction

equally important ideas

Some conjunctions link words or groups of words which add extra meaning but which are less important than the rest of the sentence.

Examples of this type of conjunction:

after although as because if that when while

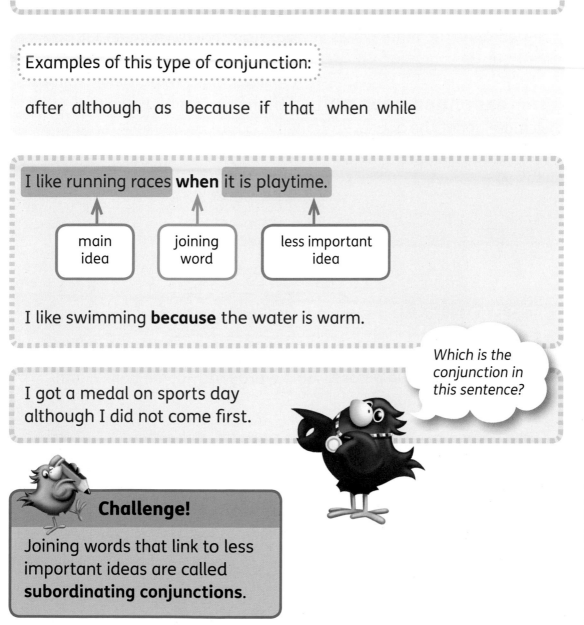

I like running races **when** it is playtime.

| main idea | joining word | less important idea |

I like swimming **because** the water is warm.

I got a medal on sports day although I did not come first.

Which is the conjunction in this sentence?

Challenge!

Joining words that link to less important ideas are called **subordinating conjunctions**.

Noun phrase

A **noun phrase** is a group of words that has a noun as its key word. All the other words in the phrase tell us more about the noun.

In an **expanded noun phrase** there are lots of words that tell us more about the noun.

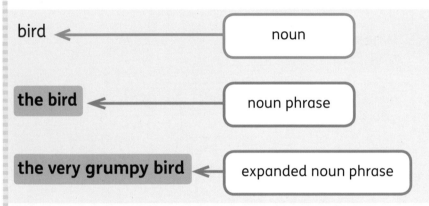

bird ← noun

the bird ← noun phrase

the very grumpy bird ← expanded noun phrase

In an expanded noun phrase, some words may come before and after the main noun.

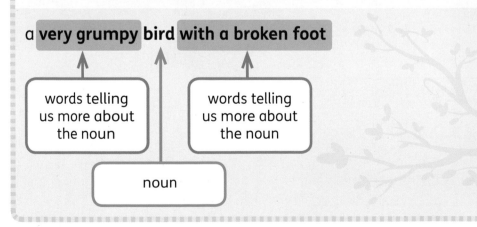

a **very grumpy** bird **with a broken foot**

words telling us more about the noun

words telling us more about the noun

noun

More noun phrases:

a greedy bird

the three bears

the red cricket ball by the fence

that steep hill

all those trains at the station

my new trainers with blue laces

Watch out!

A noun phrase *never* has a verb.

Challenge!

A **phrase** is a group of words that makes sense. It always has one main word. If that main word is a verb, we call it a clause.

Tense

Every verb in a sentence has a **tense**. It tells us when something happens.

Present tense

The **present tense** tells us that something happens now. It usually has no ending, or it ends with **-s**.

I **like** bananas.

present tense verb

The bird **pecks** the apples.

Which is the present tense verb in this sentence?

This apple **smells** bad.

Challenge!

If the verb ends in **-s**, **-ss**, **-x**, **-sh** or **-ch**, the suffix **-es** is used instead of **-s**.

Dad **mixes** the paint.
The kite **crashes** to the ground.
The girl **watches** the kite in the sky.

Grammar

Present progressive tense

The **present progressive tense** tells us that something is still happening now. It is on-going. It is a present tense.

It is made up of two verbs. The first verb is **am, is** or **are**. The second verb ends with the suffix **-ing**.

I **am enjoying** this ice cream.

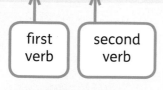

first verb

second verb

See page 60 for more about adding -ing to verbs.

The bird **is flying** away.

They **are leaving** early.

Challenge!

The verbs **am, are** and **is** are all forms of the verb **be**. They are all in the present tense. We call these verbs **auxiliary verbs** (or 'helping verbs') when they are used like this in the progressive tenses.

Past tense

The **past tense** tells us that something happened earlier. It usually ends with the suffix **-ed**.

The bird **pecked** the apple.

past tense verb

I **dropped** my bag.

We **played** football.

See pages 60-61 for more about adding **-ed** to verbs.

Watch out!

Some verbs change completely in the past tense.

do → did
eat → ate
go → went
is → was
think → thought

See page 32 for more on tricky past tense verbs.

Grammar

Past progressive tense

The **past progressive tense** tells us that something was happening. It was not finished or was still happening when something else happened. It is a past tense.

It is made up of two verbs. The first verb is **was** or **were**. The second verb ends with the suffix **-ing**.

I **was playing** a game.

first verb

second verb

We **were eating** when the doorbell rang.

I was running to school when I dropped my glove.

Which words are in the past progressive tense in this sentence?

Challenge!

The verbs **was** and **were** are both forms of the verb **be**. They are in the past tense. We call these verbs **auxiliary verbs** (or 'helping verbs') when they are used like this in the progressive tenses.

Past progressive tense

31

Tricky past tense verbs

Some verbs in the past tense do not end in **-ed**. They may change completely, or take a different ending.

present tense	past tense
am	was
are	were
bend	bent
bite	bit
break	broke
buy	bought
catch	caught
creep	crept
dig	dug
do	did
eat	ate
go	went

present tense	past tense
have	had
hear	heard
hide	hid
is	was
meet	met
see	saw
sell	sold
sleep	slept
spend	spent
take	took
tell	told
think	thought

*What is the past tense of the word **fly**?*

Grammar

Using the same tense

When you are writing, it is important to keep to the same tense. If you are writing about something that happened in the **past**, you need to use **past tense verbs**.

Leo **dropped** the plate and it **broke**.
Mum **shouted** and the dog **barked**.

If you are writing about something that is happening now, in the **present**, you need to use **present tense verbs**.

Leo **drops** the plate and it **breaks**.
Mum **shouts** and the dog **barks**.

Amir walks to school and meets his friend.

*How would you make this sentence **past tense**?*

Good writing

When you are writing sentences, try to use interesting words.

The words in purple are very common words. We often use them too much. Try to use other words that are more interesting in your own writing.

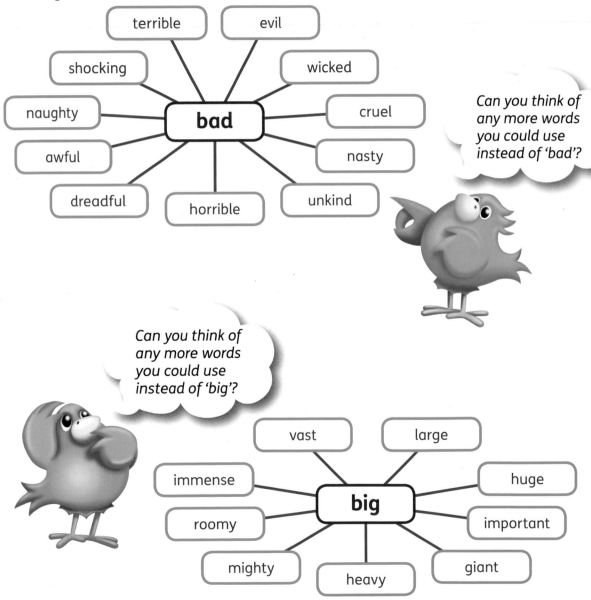

Can you think of any more words you could use instead of 'bad'?

Can you think of any more words you could use instead of 'big'?

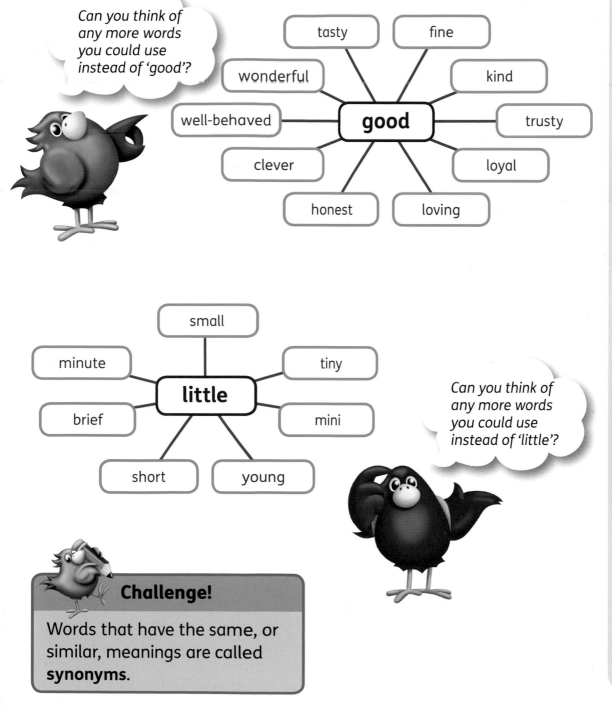

Can you think of any more words you could use instead of 'good'?

tasty · fine · wonderful · kind · well-behaved · **good** · trusty · clever · loyal · honest · loving

small · minute · tiny · **little** · brief · mini · short · young

Can you think of any more words you could use instead of 'little'?

Challenge!

Words that have the same, or similar, meanings are called **synonyms**.

Grammar

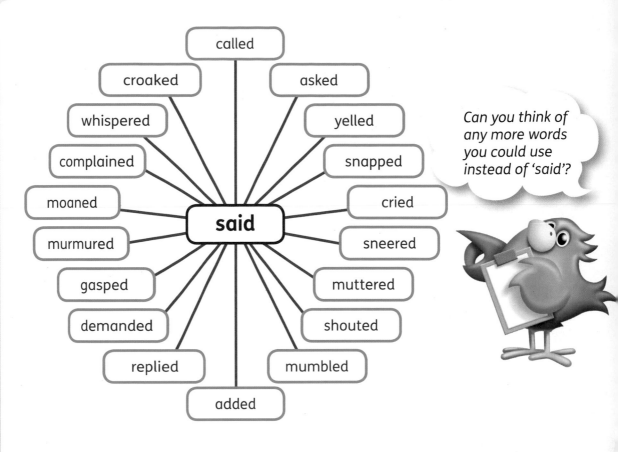

called

croaked

asked

whispered

yelled

complained

snapped

moaned

cried

said

murmured

sneered

gasped

muttered

demanded

shouted

replied

mumbled

added

Can you think of any more words you could use instead of 'said'?

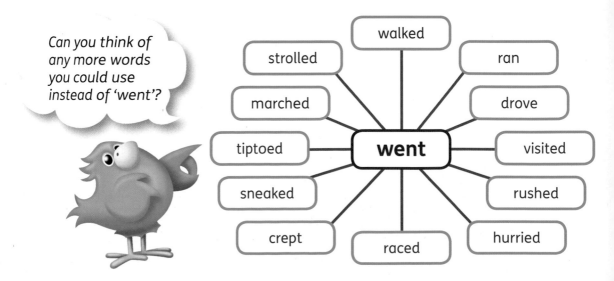

Can you think of any more words you could use instead of 'went'?

walked

strolled

ran

marched

drove

tiptoed

went

visited

sneaked

rushed

crept

hurried

raced

36

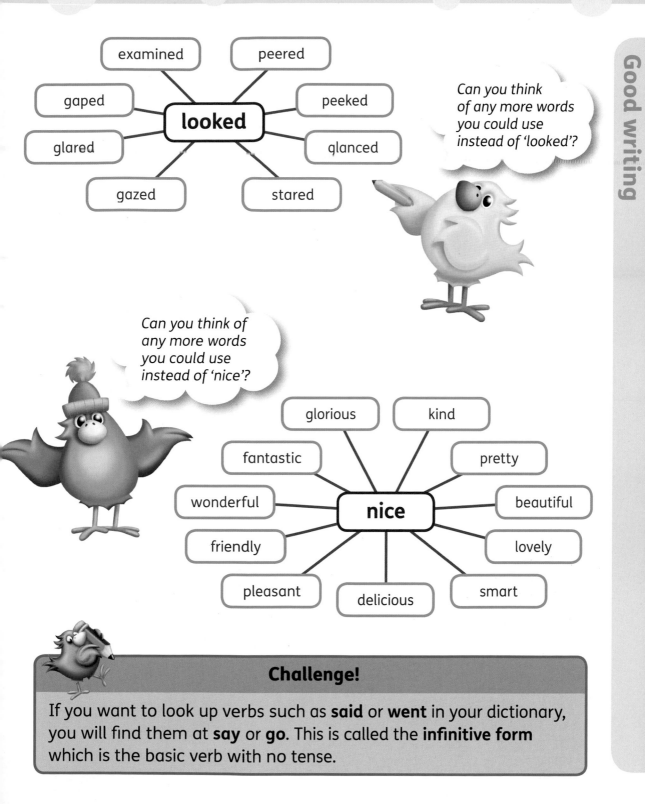

examined

peered

gaped

peeked

looked

glared

glanced

gazed

stared

Can you think of any more words you could use instead of 'looked'?

Can you think of any more words you could use instead of 'nice'?

glorious

kind

fantastic

pretty

wonderful

nice

beautiful

friendly

lovely

pleasant

smart

delicious

Challenge!

If you want to look up verbs such as **said** or **went** in your dictionary, you will find them at **say** or **go**. This is called the **infinitive form** which is the basic verb with no tense.

Punctuation

Punctuation marks help us to read sentences and to understand them.

They are like signposts. They tell us:
- ★ where a sentence begins
- ★ where a sentence ends
- ★ where you should slow down or pause
- ★ where someone is speaking
- ★ where someone is asking a question
- ★ where someone is exclaiming (showing surprise or emotion).

What do these punctuation marks tell us?

Challenge!

Sentences can mean different things if they have different punctuation.

Let's eat Granny!

Let's eat, Granny!

The comma shows that Granny is being spoken to. Without the comma, it looks like Granny is lunch!

Capital letter

A **capital letter** should be at the beginning of every sentence.

These birds are friends.

capital letter

See page 9 for more on capital letters.

This little bird is sad.

Now all the birds are happy.

We also use capital letters to name a particular person, place or thing.

People: **L**ola, **Q**ueen **E**lizabeth, **M**r **B**rown, **F**reddie

Places: **S**cotland, **A**frica, **P**aris, **F**rance

See page 14 for more about proper nouns.

Games: **M**inecraft, **A**ngry **B**irds, **C**onnect 4

Books and films: **T**he **G**ruffalo, **P**addington, **M**adagascar

Watch out!

We always use a capital letter for the pronoun I, even if it is in the middle of a sentence.

Yesterday, **I** went swimming.

Full stop

This is a **full stop**  . It comes at the end of a sentence. It shows that a sentence is finished.

This is a sentence.

full stop

More full stops:

I am six.

This is my sister.

My friend Noah is seven.

We like playing at the park.

We climb trees and run races.

Sometimes we get wet and muddy.

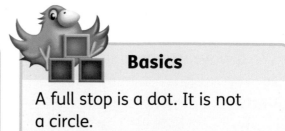

Basics

Do not leave a space between the final letter and full stop.

Basics

A full stop is a dot. It is not a circle.

Punctuation

Question mark

This is a **question mark** ? . It comes at the end of a sentence which asks a question.

Are you coming**?**

question mark

More question marks:

Where are you**?**

Who was that**?**

Do you like cheese**?**

What time is it**?**

Exclamation mark

This is an **exclamation mark** ! . It comes at the end of a sentence which shows that something is being exclaimed or said with a lot of feeling. Exclamations often start with the words 'what' or 'how'.

What a great party**!**

How fantastic**!**

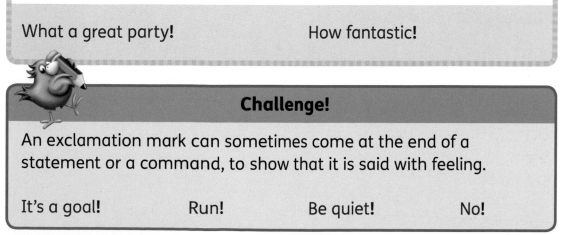

Challenge!

An exclamation mark can sometimes come at the end of a statement or a command, to show that it is said with feeling.

It's a goal**!**

Run**!**

Be quiet**!**

No**!**

Comma

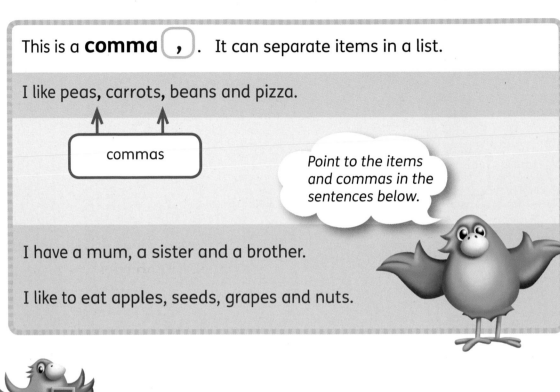

This is a **comma** (,). It can separate items in a list.

I like peas, carrots, beans and pizza.

commas

Point to the items and commas in the sentences below.

I have a mum, a sister and a brother.

I like to eat apples, seeds, grapes and nuts.

Basics

A comma starts on the same line as the letters. Then it dips just below the line.

the dog, cat and bird ✔

the dog' cat and bird ✘

Punctuation

A **comma** can come before a conjunction that links two parts of a sentence.

I like milk, but I love juice!

> comma before the joining word 'but'

We are eating tea, and then we will play outside.
Did you draw this, or did someone help you?

A **comma** can separate the name of the person being spoken to from the rest of the sentence.

Mum, I'm home!   Dinner is ready, Jess.

I like strawberry ice cream although I don't really like strawberries.

Danny do you want to play football?

> *Where would you put the comma in each of these sentences?*

Challenge!

If the name of the person being spoken to is in the middle of a sentence, it needs a comma before and after it.

When your room is tidy, **Zoe,** you can ask Tilly to play.

> two commas, one name

Apostrophe

An **apostrophe** (') can show that letters are missing from a word.

It's an angry bird.

apostrophe

Challenge!

Words that are shortened by missing out some letters are called **contractions**.

I don't like sprouts.

I'll have yours.

Which letters are missing in the shortened words?

More apostrophes in shortened words:

she'll	=	she will	he'd	= he had or he would
they've	=	they have	we're	= we are
you're	=	you are	didn't	= did not
doesn't	=	does not	shouldn't	= should not

Watch out!

It is easy to confuse **your** and **you're**. If you can say the words 'you are' instead of 'your' in a sentence, then you should use an apostrophe.

It is also easy to confuse **its** and **it's**. If you can say the words 'it is' or 'it has' instead of 'its' in a sentence, then you should use an apostrophe.

Punctuation

An apostrophe can show that something belongs to someone. This is called a **possessive apostrophe**. It is used with the letter **s** on the end of some words.

the boy**'s** pen (the pen belonging to the boy)

↑
possessive apostrophe

If the word ends in **–ss**, still add **'s**.

the princess**'s** crown

Challenge!

If the word is plural and ends in **–s**, just add **'**.
the girls**'** bags (the bags belonging to the girls)

If the word is plural and does not end in **–s**, add **'s**.
the children**'s** shoes (the shoes belonging to the children)

Spelling

Spelling can be tricky! To spell well, you need to think about how each word sounds and what letters can make those sounds.

There are 26 letters in the alphabet, but there are 44 sounds in the English language. This means that although each letter on its own can make one sound, we need two or more letters to make some of the other sounds in our language.

See page 8 for more about the alphabet.

For example, the letter **s** makes the sound **/s/** as in **s**at.

The letter **h** makes the sound **/h/** as in **h**at.

If we put these letters together, they can make a different sound **/sh/** as in **sh**op.

In this part of the book, you will find out more about letters and sounds. You will also find some rules to help you spell words correctly.

Vowels and consonants

The letters **a e i o u** are called **vowel letters**.
These vowels can make a short vowel sound or a long vowel sound.
All the other letters in the alphabet are called **consonant letters**.

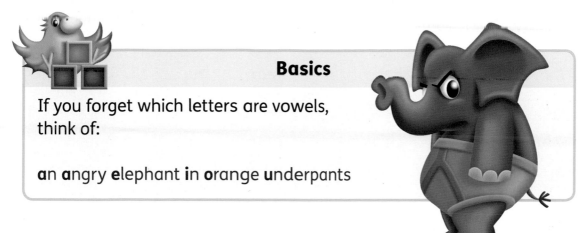

Basics

If you forget which letters are vowels,
think of:

an **a**ngry **e**lephant **i**n **o**range **u**nderpants

How to spell the short vowel sounds

The short vowel sounds are spelt with just one letter.

The sound **/a/** as in **a**nt is spelt with **a**.

The sound **/e/** as in h**e**n is spelt with **e**.

The sound **/i/** as in **i**nsect is spelt with **i**.

The sound **/o/** as in **o**range is spelt with **o**.

The sound **/u/** as in **u**mbrella is spelt with **u**.

How to spell consonant sounds

Most consonant sounds are spelt with one consonant letter, but some are spelt with two.

sound	letter(s)	as in...
/b/	b	**b**at
/c/	c, k	**c**ake
/ch/	ch	**ch**ips
/d/	d	**d**ig
/f/	f	**f**ish
/g/	g	**g**orilla
/h/	h	**h**at
/j/	J	**j**elly
/l/	l	**l**eg
/m/	m	**m**ice
/n/	n	**n**et

sound	letter(s)	as in...
/ng/	ng	ki**ng**
/p/	p	**p**in
/qu/	qu	**qu**een
/r/	r	**r**at
/s/	s	**s**un
/t/	t	**t**ent
/th/	th	**th**in
/v/	v	**v**et
/w/	w	**w**in
/x/	x	exit
/y/	y	**y**ell
/z/	z	**z**ip

How to spell the long vowel sounds

The sound /ay/ as in day

There are many ways of spelling this sound:

ay	day	play
a_e	cake	same
ai	train	rain
a	acorn	angel

Watch out!

There are a few common words that use **ea** to make the sound **/ay/**:

br**ea**k   gr**ea**t

Vowel sounds

The sound /ee/ as in tree

There are many ways of spelling this sound:

ee	tree	peel
e_e	these	compete
ey	key	monkey
ie	thief	field
ea	sea	meat

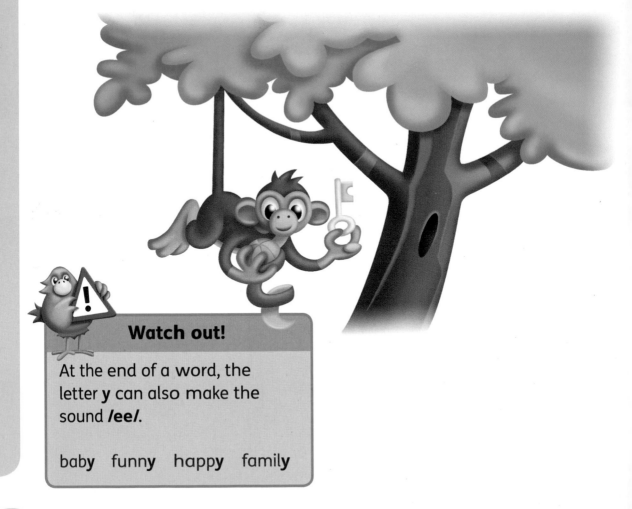

Watch out!

At the end of a word, the letter **y** can also make the sound **/ee/**.

baby   funny   happy   family

Spelling

Vowel sounds

The sound /igh/ as in high

There are many ways of spelling this sound:

igh	high	night
ie	pie	tie
i-e	kite	slide
i	mind	find

Watch out!

In a few words, the letter **y** can also make the sound **/igh/**.

fly   my   July   cry

The sound /oa/ as in boat

There are many ways of spelling this sound:

oa	boat	coat
o-e	home	broke
ow	snow	grow
oe	toe	goes
o	so	go

51

The sound /oo/ as in zoo

There are many ways of spelling this sound:

oo	zoo	moon
u_e	flute	rule
ue	blue	true
ew	crew	flew
o	to	who

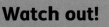

Watch out!

The sound **/oo/** (above) and the sound **/yoo/** (below) can both be spelt **u_e**, **ue** and **ew**.

The sound /yoo/ as in tune

There are many ways of spelling this sound:

u_e	tune	cube
ue	argue	rescue
ew	knew	new
u	tuna	useful

Spelling

More vowel sounds

sound	examples
short /oo/	book could push
short /e/	head bread
short /o/	want squash
short /uh/	mother nothing Monday
/ar/	car father
/or/	fork saw your dinosaur floor more war reward water walk all
/ur/	burn her bird worm
/ou/	clown sound
/oi/	coin toy
/ear/	year beard
/eer/	hear deer
/air/	chair care bear there
/er/ ('schwa' sound)	sister winter better
/yoor/	sure

More consonant sounds

Spelling rule

The sounds **/f/, /l/, /s/, /z/** and **/k/** are usually spelt **ff, ll, ss, zz** and **ck** when they are used after a single vowel in a short word.

o**ff**   we**ll**   hi**ss**   bu**zz**   ba**ck**

Watch out!

Not all words follow the rule above:
bus   if   pal   yes   us

Spelling rule

The sound **/k/** is spelt with a **k** rather than a **c** before the letters **e**, **i** and **y**.

kennel   **ki**t   fris**ky**

Say the word 'front' then 'trunk'. Think how your tongue moves to a different place in your mouth for each 'n' sound.

Watch out!

When the letter **n** comes before **k**, the sound **/n/** is a bit different. It sounds more like the **n** in **/ng/**.
ba**nk**   su**nk**   thi**nk**

Spelling

Spelling rule

The sound **/f/** can be spelt **ph**.

alp**ph**abet   ele**ph**ant   dol**ph**in

Basics

Most short words use the letter
f to spell the sound **/f/**.
fun   **f**ill   **f**at

Spelling rule

Many words use the letters **wh** to make the sound **/w/**.

when   **wh**eel   **wh**ere

Spelling rule

Words that end with the sound **/v/**, usually end with the spelling **-ve**.

gi**ve**   ha**ve**   li**ve**

Spelling rule

The spelling **-tch** usually comes after a single vowel letter.
(The letter **t** is silent.)

ca**tch**   ki**tch**en   hu**tch**

Spelling

Spelling rule

At the end of a word, the letter **j** is never used to spell the sound **/j/**. Instead, we use **-dge** or **-ge**.

ba**dge**   bri**dge**   fu**dge**   a**ge**   villa**ge**   hu**ge**

The sound **/j/** is spelt **g** at the start or in the middle of words.

giant   **g**iraffe   ma**g**ic

Basics

The sound **/j/** is always spelt **j** before the vowels **a**, **o** and **u**.

jar   **j**og   **j**acket

Spelling rule

The sound **/s/** is spelt **c** before **e**, **i** and **y**.

ra**ce**   **ci**ty   fan**cy**

Spelling rule

The letter **s** can make a **/zh/** sound.

televi**s**ion   u**s**ual   trea**s**ure

Silent letters

Some words have silent letters. The letters **k**, **g** and **w** are always silent when written at the start of a word before a consonant.

knee   **k**now   **g**naw   **g**nat   **w**rite   **w**rap

*A silent letter has no sound when we **say** the word.*

Words ending -le, -el, -al and -il

At the end of words, the sound **/l/** is usually spelt **-le**.

app**le**   tab**le**   litt**le**

The **-el** spelling is used after **m**, **n**, **r**, **s**, **v** and **w**.

cam**el**   flann**el**   squirr**el**   weas**el**   lev**el**   tow**el**

A few nouns end **-al**.

anim**al**   ped**al**   hospit**al**   crimin**al**

There are a few words that end **-il**.

penc**il**   foss**il**   gerb**il**

Adding -ing, -ed and -er

If a word ends with two consonant letters (the same or different), then the endings **-ing**, **-ed** or **-er** are just added on.

See page 47 for more about consonants.

Challenge!

A word that can make sense on its own is called a **root word**. **Suffixes** and **prefixes** can be added to root words.

help + **ing** = help**ing**			jump + **ing** = jump**ing**	
help + **ed** = help**ed**			jump + **ed** = jump**ed**	
help + **er** = help**er**			jump + **er** = jump**er**	

Add the same endings to the word 'buzz'.

Adding -er and -est to adjectives

*I am **tall**.*

*I am tall**er**.*

*I am tall**est**.*

If an adjective ends with two consonant letters (the same or different), then the endings **-er** and **-est** are just added on.

We use the ending **-er** when two things are being compared. This is called the **comparative**.

quick + **er** = quick**er**	tall + **er** = tall**er**
fast + **er** = fast**er**	short + **er** = short**er**

We use the ending **-est** when more than two things are being compared. This is called the **superlative**.

quick + **est** = quick**est**	tall + **est** = tall**est**
fast + **est** = fast**est**	short + **est** = short**est**

Watch out!

Some adjectives use **more** and **most** to make the comparative and superlative.

interesting	more interesting	most interesting
beautiful	more beautiful	most beautiful

Adding -ed, -er, -est and -ing to words ending in -y

If a word ends with a consonant and a **-y**, change the **-y** to **i** and then add **-ed**, **-er** or **-est**.

cry   → **i** + **ed** = cr**ied**
reply   → **i** + **ed** = repl**ied**
try   → **i** + **ed** = tr**ied**

funny → **i** + **er** = funn**ier**
shiny → **i** + **er** = shin**ier**
wobbly → **i** + **er** = wobbl**ier**

funny → **i** + **est** = funn**iest**
shiny → **i** + **est** = shin**iest**
wobbly → **i** + **est** = wobbl**iest**

How would you add the endings -er and -est to the word 'happy'?

Watch out!

When adding **-ing** to words ending with a consonant and **-y**, do not change the **y** to and **i**, but simply add the **-ing** to the end of the word.

cry**ing**   reply**ing**   try**ing**

The only common words with **ii** in are sk**ii**ng and tax**ii**ng.

Adding -ed, -ing, -er and -est to words ending in -e

If a word ends with **-e**, the **-e** is dropped before the ending is added.

hike → + **ing** = hik**ing**
hike → + **ed** = hik**ed**
hike → + **er** = hik**er**

rude → + **er** = rud**er**
rude → + **est** = rud**est**

nice → + **er** = nic**er**
nice → + **est** = nic**est**

How would you add the endings -er and -est to the word 'late'?

Watch out!

When you add **-ing** to the word 'be', the **e** is never dropped.

be → + **ing** = be**ing**

Syllables

A **syllable** is like a 'beat' in a spoken word.

Some words have one syllable:

| you | bike | ball | tree | bird | peas |

Some words have two syllables:

| pocket | singing | boxes | football | rabbit |

Some words have three syllables:

| elephant | dinosaur | understand | family |

Basics

Clap the rhythm of a word, to check how many syllables it has. One clap means one syllable.

*How many syllables are in the word **hippopotamus**?*

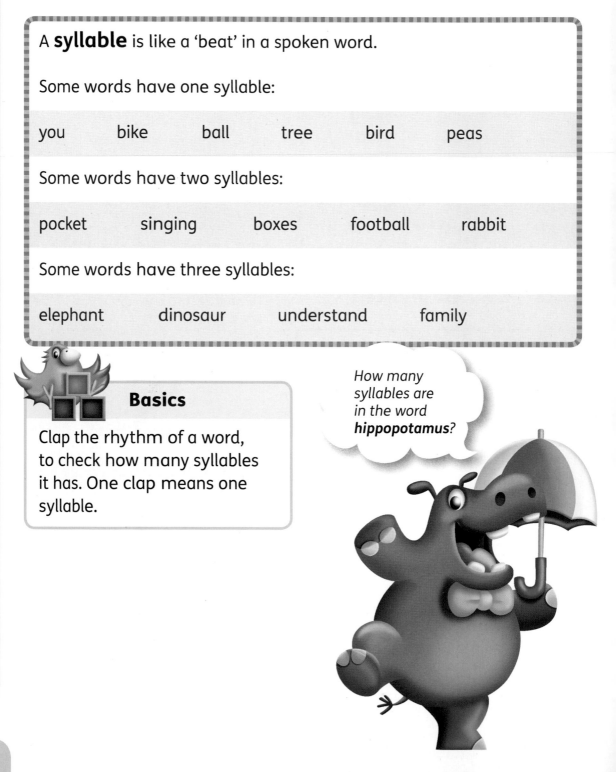

Adding endings and doubling letters

When adding an ending to a word of one syllable, which ends in a vowel and a consonant, the consonant is doubled.

sad   + **d** + **er** = sad**der**
fat   + **t** + **est** = fat**test**

pat   + **t** + **ing** = pat**ting**
drop + **p** + **ed** = drop**ped**
drum + **m** + **er** = drum**mer**
run   + **n** + **y**   = run**ny**

*How would you make the verb **hum** into the past tense?*

Watch out!

The letter **x** is never doubled.

mixer   boxed   fixing   foxes

Prefixes

A **prefix** is a group of letters that is added to the beginning of a word. This makes a new word.

The prefix **un-** changes words to mean the opposite.

un + well   = **un**well
un + happy = **un**happy
un + do   = **un**do
un + fair   = **un**fair
un + lock = **un**lock
un + kind = **un**kind

Challenge!

Other prefixes with different meanings:

prefix	meaning	example
super–	greater, above	**super**hero
anti–	against	**anti**clockwise
sub–	below	**sub**marine
bi–	two, twice	**bi**cycle

Suffixes to make nouns

A **suffix** is a group of letters that is added to the end of a word. Some suffixes are added to words to make nouns. The most common are **-ment** and **-ness**.

enjoy + **ment** = enjoy**ment**
pay + **ment** = pay**ment**
agree + **ment** = agree**ment**

sad + **ness** = sad**ness**
bold + **ness** = bold**ness**
cool + **ness** = cool**ness**

Watch out!

Some words that end in **-y** change the **y** into **i** before adding the suffix.

merry → **i** + **ment** = merr**iment**
happy → **i** + **ness** = happ**iness**

Suffixes to make adjectives

Some suffixes are added to words to make adjectives. The most common are **-ness** and **-ful**.

The suffix **-less** means to be without something.

hope + **less** = hope**less**
care + **less** = care**less**
fear + **less** = fear**less**

The suffix **-ful** means to be full of something.

hope + **ful** = hope**ful**
care + **ful** = care**ful**
fear + **ful** = fear**ful**

*How would you turn the word **colour** into an adjective?*

Watch out!

The suffix **-ful** just has one **l**.
The word 'full' has two **l**s.

Suffixes to make adverbs

The suffix **-ly** can be added to words to make adverbs.

bad   + **ly** = bad**ly**
soft   + **ly** = soft**ly**
sudden   + **ly** = sudden**ly**

Watch out!

Some words ending in **-y** need to change the **y** into **i** before adding the suffix **-ly**.

happy → **i** + **ly** = happ**ily**
angry → **i** + **ly** = angr**ily**

Words ending in –tion

Some words end with the sound '*shun*'.
This sound is often spelt **-tion**.

ac**tion**   sta**tion**   sec**tion**   na**tion**   fic**tion**

Compound words

> A **compound word** is made up of two words joined together.
>
> super + **man** = super**man**
> foot + **ball** = foot**ball**
> bed + **room** = bed**room**
> white + **board** = white**board**

More compound words:

starfish	firefighter	haircut	blackbird
bookshop	snowflake	outgrow	goalkeeper
farmyard	blackberry		

Can you make three compound words out of these words?

rain	after	end
week	noon	bow

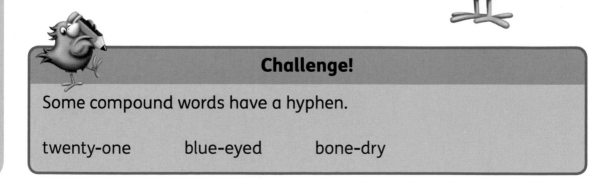

Challenge!

Some compound words have a hyphen.

twenty-one   blue-eyed   bone-dry

Tricky spellings

Group 1					
a	are	ask	be	by	come
do	friend	full	go	has	he
here	his	house	I	is	love
me	my	no	once	one	to
today	of	our	pull	push	put
said	says	school	she	so	some
the	there	they	was	we	were
where	you	your			

Group 2					
again	after	any	bath	beautiful	because
behind	both	break	busy	child	children
Christmas	class	climb	clothes	cold	could
door	even	every	everybody	eye	fast
father	find	floor	gold	grass	great
half	hold	hour	improve	kind	last
many	mind	money	most	move	Mr
Mrs	old	only	parents	pass	past
path	people	plant	poor	pretty	prove
should	steak	sugar	sure	told	water
who	whole	wild	would		

Try to learn these words so that you know how to spell them.

Homophones

> **Homophones** are words that sound the same but have different spellings and meanings.
>
> It is easy to get homophones mixed up!
> Check you are using the right word when you are writing.

*My **new** friend.*

*I **knew** it would be fun having a friend.*

here	hear		see	sea
bare	bear		one	won
sun	son		be	bee
blue	blew		night	knight

Watch out!

Learn these homophones:

I am going **to** the circus.	→	**To** shows a direction.
I would like to go **too**.	→	**Too** means as well.
I will book **two** tickets.	→	**Two** is a number.

Spelling

Watch out!

Learn these homophones:

It is **their** dog.	→	**Their** means it belongs to them.
They're walking the dog.	→	**They're** means 'they are'.
There is the dog.	→	**There** shows a place.

Challenge!

More homophones:

berry	bury	brake	break
groan	grown	heel	heal
here	hear	know	no
meat	meet	peace	piece
plain	plane	scene	seen
weather	whether	whose	who's

Two words that are often mixed up are **quite** and **quiet**. These words sound similar, but not the same.

Say 'quite' and 'quiet' slowly. Can you hear the difference?

How to use this dictionary

How to use this dictionary

This dictionary helps with spelling tricky words. The words have been chosen by looking at the national curriculum and the findings from the *Oxford Children's Corpus*. It includes the words children often misspell and which they need to know for school.

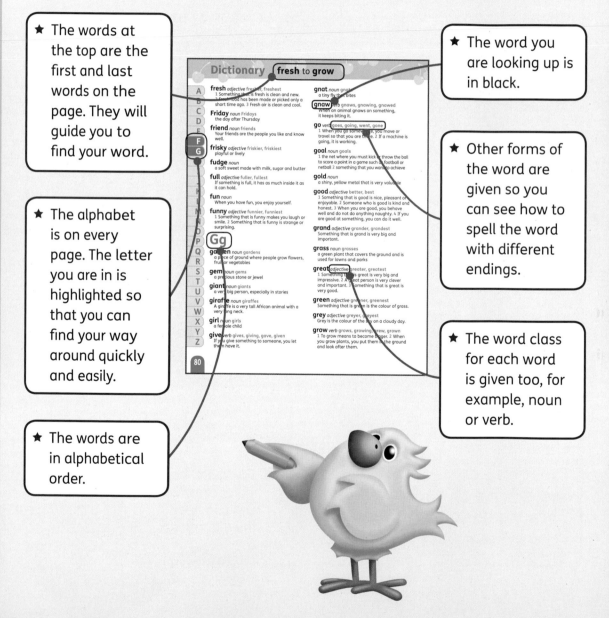

★ The words at the top are the first and last words on the page. They will guide you to find your word.

★ The alphabet is on every page. The letter you are in is highlighted so that you can find your way around quickly and easily.

★ The words are in alphabetical order.

★ The word you are looking up is in black.

★ Other forms of the word are given so you can see how to spell the word with different endings.

★ The word class for each word is given too, for example, noun or verb.

Dictionary — fresh to grow

fresh *adjective* fresher, freshest
1 Something that is fresh is clean and new. 2 Fresh food has been made or picked only a short time ago. 3 Fresh air is clean and cool.

Friday *noun* Fridays
the day after Thursday

friend *noun* friends
Your friends are the people you like and know well.

frisky *adjective* friskier, friskiest
playful or lively

fudge *noun*
a soft sweet made with milk, sugar and butter

full *adjective* fuller, fullest
If something is full, it has as much inside it as it can hold.

fun *noun*
When you have fun, you enjoy yourself.

funny *adjective* funnier, funniest
1 Something that is funny makes you laugh or smile. 2 Something that is funny is strange or surprising.

Gg

garden *noun* gardens
a place of ground where people grow flowers, fruit or vegetables

gem *noun* gems
a precious stone or jewel

giant *noun* giants
a very big person, especially in stories

giraffe *noun* giraffes
A giraffe is a very tall African animal with a very long neck.

girl *noun* girls
a female child

give *verb* gives, giving, gave, given
If you give something to someone, you let them have it.

gnat *noun* gnats
a tiny fly that bites

gnaw *verb* gnaws, gnawing, gnawed
When an animal gnaws on something, it keeps biting it.

go *verb* goes, going, went, gone
1 When you go somewhere, you move or travel so that you are there. 2 If a machine is going, it is working.

goal *noun* goals
1 the net where you must kick or throw the ball to score a point in a game such as football or netball 2 something that you want to achieve

gold *noun*
a shiny, yellow metal that is very valuable

good *adjective* better, best
1 Something that is good is nice, pleasant or enjoyable. 2 Someone who is good is kind and honest. 3 When you are good, you behave well and do not do anything naughty. 4 If you are good at something, you can do it well.

grand *adjective* grander, grandest
Something that is grand is very big and important.

grass *noun* grasses
a green plant that covers the ground and is used for lawns and parks

great *adjective* greater, greatest
1 Something that is great is very big and impressive. 2 A great person is very clever and important. 3 Something that is great is very good.

green *adjective* greener, greenest
Something that is green is the colour of grass.

grey *adjective* greyer, greyest
Grey is the colour of the sky on a cloudy day.

grow *verb* grows, growing, grew, grown
1 To grow means to become bigger. 2 When you grow plants, you put them in the ground and look after them.

80

Aa

accident *noun* **accidents**
1 When there is an accident, something bad happens and someone gets hurt.
2 If something that you did was an accident, you did not do it on purpose.

accidentally *adverb*
When you do something accidentally, you did not do it on purpose.

adjective *noun* **adjectives**
An adjective gives more information about a noun.

adjust *verb* **adjusts, adjusting, adjusted**
To adjust something is to change it slightly or change its position.

adverb *noun* **adverbs**
An adverb gives more information about a verb.

afraid *adjective*
If you are afraid, you are frightened.

again *adverb*
once more

age *noun*
Your age is how old you are.

air *noun*
Air is the gas all around us, which we breathe.

alphabet *noun* **alphabets**
all the letters that we use in writing, arranged in a particular order

always *adverb*
at all times or every time

animal *noun* **animals**
An animal is anything that lives and can move about. Birds, fish, snakes, wasps and elephants are all animals.

annoy *verb* **annoys, annoying, annoyed**
If something annoys you, it makes you angry.

any
some

apple *noun* **apples**
a round, crisp, juicy fruit

April *noun*
the fourth month of the year

argument *noun* **arguments**
a quarrel

arm *noun* **arms**
Your arms are the long parts of your body that are joined to your shoulders.

around *adverb*
all round

ask *verb* **asks, asking, asked**
1 If you ask someone a question, you say it to them so that they will tell you the answer.
2 If you ask for something, you say that you want it.

astronaut *noun* **astronauts**
someone who travels in space

August *noun*
the eighth month of the year

author *noun* **authors**
someone who writes books or stories

autumn *noun* **autumns**
the time of year when leaves fall off the trees and it gets colder

Bb

baby *noun* **babies**
a very young child

back *noun* **backs**
1 Your back is the part of your body that is behind you, between your neck and your bottom. 2 An animal's back is the long part of its body between its head and its tail.
3 The back of something is the part opposite the front.

a
b
c
d
e
f
g
h
i
j
k
l
m
n
o
p
q
r
s
t
u
v
w
x
y
z

A B C D E F G H I J K L M N O P Q R S T U V W X Y Z

back *adverb*
If you go back to a place, you go there again.

badge *noun* **badges**
a small thing that you pin or sew on to your clothes, to show which school or club you belong to

badly *adverb*
1 If you do something badly, you do not do it very well. 2 If you are badly hurt or upset, you are hurt or upset a lot.

ball *noun* **balls**
1 a round object that you hit, kick or throw in games 2 a big party where people wear very smart clothes and dance with each other

bank *noun* **banks**
1 A bank is a place where people can keep their money safely. Banks also lend money to people. 2 the ground near the edge of a river or lake

bare *adjective* **barer, barest**
1 If a part of your body is bare, it has nothing covering it. 2 If something is bare, it has nothing on it or in it.

bath *noun* **baths**
a large container which you can fill with water to sit in and wash yourself all over

be *verb* **I am, you are, he/she/it is, we/they are, I/he/she/it was, you were, we/they were**
1 To be is to exist or happen. 2 To be someone or something is to have that position or quality.

bear *noun* **bears**
a large wild animal with thick fur and sharp teeth and claws

bear *verb* **bears, bearing, bore, borne**
1 If something will bear your weight, it will support your weight and so you can stand on it safely. 2 If you cannot bear something, you hate it.

beard *noun* **beards**
hair growing on a man's chin

beautiful *adjective*
1 Something that is beautiful is very nice to look at, hear or smell. 2 Someone who is beautiful has a lovely face.

because *conjunction*
for the reason that

bedroom *noun* **bedrooms**
a room where you sleep

bee *noun* **bees**
A bee is an insect that can fly and sting you.

before *adverb*
earlier than

behind *adverb*
at or to the back of something

believe *verb* **believes, believing, believed**
If you believe something, you feel that it is true.

better *adjective*
1 If one thing is better than another, it is more interesting, more useful or more exciting. 2 If you are better than someone else, you are able to do something more quickly or more successfully. 3 When you are better, you are well again after an illness.

bird *noun* **birds**
any animal with feathers, wings and a beak

black *adjective* **blacker, blackest**
Something that is black is the colour of the sky on a very dark night.

blackberry *noun* **blackberries**
a sweet black berry

blow *noun* **blows**
If you receive a blow, someone hits you hard.

blow *verb* **blows, blowing, blew, blown**
1 When you blow, you make air come out of your mouth. 2 When the wind blows, it moves along.

blue *adjective* **bluer, bluest**
Something that is blue is the colour of the sky on a fine day.

boat *noun* **boats**
something that floats on water and can carry people and things over water

book *noun* **books**
a set of pages that are joined together inside a cover

born *adjective*
When a baby is born, it comes out of its mother's body and starts to live.

bottle *noun* **bottles**
a tall glass or plastic container that you keep liquids in

boxer *noun* **boxers**
someone who boxes

boy *noun* **boys**
a male child

bread *noun*
a food that is made from flour and water and baked in the oven

break *verb* **breaks, breaking, broke, broken**
1 If you break something, you smash it into several pieces. 2 If you break something, you damage it so that it no longer works. 3 If you break a law or a promise, you do something that goes against it. 4 If something breaks down, it stops working.

bridge *noun* **bridges**
something that is built over a river, railway or road so that people can go across it

bright *adjective* **brighter, brightest**
1 A bright light shines with a lot of light.
2 A bright colour is strong and not dull.
3 A bright day is sunny. 4 Someone who is bright is clever and learns things quickly.

brother *noun* **brothers**
Your brother is a boy who has the same parents as you.

brown *adjective* **browner, brownest**
Something that is brown is the colour of soil.

bulge *verb* **bulges, bulging, bulged**
If something bulges, it sticks out because it is so full.

burst *verb* **bursts, bursting, burst**
If something bursts, it suddenly breaks open.

bus *noun* **buses**
something that a lot of people can travel in on a road

busy *adjective* **busier, busiest**
1 If you are busy, you have a lot of things to do. 2 A busy place has a lot of people and traffic in it.

buzz *verb* **buzzes, buzzing, buzzed**
When something buzzes, it makes a sound like a bee.

buzzer *noun* **buzzers**
A buzzer is something that makes a buzzing sound, for example when you press it or when you connect it to an electric circuit.

Cc

call *verb* **calls, calling, called**
1 When you call to someone, you speak loudly so that they can hear you. 2 When you call someone, you tell them to come to you. 3 When you call someone a name, you give them that name. 4 When you call someone, you telephone them.

camel *noun* **camels**
A camel is a big animal with one or two humps on its back. Camels are used to carry people and goods in deserts, because they can travel for a long time without eating or drinking.

can *noun* **cans**
a tin with food or drink in

can *verb* **could**
If you can do something, you are able to do it.

car *noun* **cars**
something that you can drive along in on a road

a b c d e f g h i j k l m n o p q r s t u v w x y z

care *verb* **cares, caring, cared**
1 If you take care when you are doing something, you do it carefully. 2 If you take care of someone, you look after them. 3 If you care about something, it is important to you. 4 If you care for someone, you look after them.

careful *adjective*
If you are careful, you make sure that you do things safely and well so that you do not have an accident.

carry *verb* **carries, carrying, carried**
1 When you carry something, you hold it in your hands or arms and take it somewhere. 2 If you carry on doing something, you keep doing it.

carrot *noun* **carrots**
a long, thin, orange vegetable

cat *noun* **cats**
A cat is a furry animal that people often keep as a pet. Lions, tigers and leopards are large, wild cats.

catch *verb* **catches, catching, caught**
1 If you catch something that is moving through the air, you get hold of it. 2 To catch someone means to find them and take them prisoner. 3 If you catch an illness, you get it. 4 When you catch a bus or train, you get on it.

cell *noun* **cells**
1 a small room in which a prisoner is kept in a prison 2 Cells are the tiny parts that all living things are made of.

centimetre *noun* **centimetres**
We can measure length in centimetres.

chair *noun* **chairs**
a seat for one person to sit on

change *verb* **changes, changing, changed**
1 When you change something, you make it different. 2 When something changes, it becomes different. 3 When you change something, you get rid of it and get a different one instead.

change *noun* **changes**
1 Change is the money you get back when you give too much money to pay for something. 2 When there is a change, something becomes different.

character *noun* **characters**
1 a person in a story 2 Your character is the sort of person you are.

charge *noun* **charges**
A charge is the amount of money that you have to pay for something.

charge *verb* **charges, charging, charged**
1 If you charge money for something, you ask for money. 2 If you charge at someone, you rush at them suddenly.

chief *noun* **chiefs**
a leader who is in charge of other people

child *noun* **children**
a young boy or girl

chimney *noun* **chimneys**
a tall pipe that takes smoke away from a fire inside a building

circle *noun* **circles**
a round shape like a ring or wheel

city *noun* **cities**
a big town

class *noun* **classes**
a group of children who learn things together

climb *verb* **climbs, climbing, climbed**
1 To climb means to go upwards. 2 When you climb, you use your hands and feet to move over things.

clothes *noun*
the things that you wear to cover your body

clue *noun* **clues**
something that helps you to find the answer to a puzzle

coach *noun* **coaches**
1 a bus that takes people on long journeys 2 The coaches on a train are the carriages

where people sit. **3** someone who trains people in a sport

coat *noun* **coats**
1 a piece of clothing with sleeves that you wear on top of other clothes to keep warm
2 An animal's coat is the hair or fur that covers its body. **3** A coat of paint is a layer of paint.

coin *noun* **coins**
a piece of metal money

cold *adjective* **colder, coldest**
1 Something that is cold is not hot.
2 Someone who is cold is not friendly.

cold *noun* **colds**
an illness that makes you sneeze and gives you a runny nose

come *verb* **comes, coming, came, come**
1 To come to a place means to move towards it.
2 When something comes, it arrives in a place.

complete *adjective*
1 Something that is complete has all its parts and has nothing missing. **2** If something is complete, it is finished. **3** Complete means in every way.

copier *noun*
a machine for copying pages

copy *verb* **copies, copying, copied**
1 When you copy something, you write it down or draw it in the same way as it has already been written or drawn. **2** When you copy something from one file to another file on a computer, you move it to the second file but do not delete it from the first file. **3** When you copy someone, you do exactly the same as them.

crawl *verb* **crawls, crawling, crawled**
1 When you crawl, you move along on your hands and knees. **2** When a car or train crawls along, it moves very slowly.

cry *verb* **cries, crying, cried**
1 When you cry, tears come out of your eyes.
2 When you cry, you shout something.

crystal *noun* **crystals**
Crystal is found in rock. It is hard and clear like glass.

cube *noun* **cubes**
A cube is a solid square shape like the shape of a dice. Cubes have six square sides that are all the same size.

cuboid *noun* **cuboids**
A cuboid is a solid shape like a cereal box with six rectangular sides.

Dd

dare *verb* **dares, daring, dared**
1 If you dare to do something, you are brave enough to do it. **2** If you dare someone to do something, you tell them to do it to show how brave they are.

day *noun* **days**
1 a period of twenty-four hours **2** the part of the day when it is light

dear *adjective* **dearer, dearest**
1 If someone is dear to you, you love them a lot. **2** Something you write before someone's name at the start of a letter. **3** Something that is dear costs a lot of money.

December *noun*
the twelfth month of the year

diamond *noun* **diamonds**
a shape that looks like a square standing on one of its corners

dinner *noun* **dinners**
Dinner is the main meal of the day.

dinosaur *noun* **dinosaurs**
an animal like a huge lizard that lived millions of years ago

do *verb* **does, doing, did, done**
When you do something, you carry out that action.

A
B
C
D
E
F
G
H
I
J
K
L
M
N
O
P
Q
R
S
T
U
V
W
X
Y
Z

dodge *verb* **dodges, dodging, dodged**
To dodge something is to move quickly to avoid it.

dog *noun* **dogs**
A dog is an animal people often keep as a pet.

dolphin *noun* **dolphins**
A dolphin is a large animal that swims like a fish and lives in the sea. Dolphins are mammals and breathe air.

donkey *noun* **donkeys**
an animal that looks like a small horse with long ears

door *noun* **doors**
something that you can open and go through to get into a place

down *adverb*
from a higher place to a lower one

draw *verb* **draws, drawing, drew, drawn**
1 When you draw a picture, you make a picture with a pen, pencil or crayon. 2 When you draw curtains, you open them or close them. 3 When two people draw in a game, they have the same score at the end of the game.

dream *noun* **dreams**
1 things that you seem to see when you are asleep 2 something that you would like very much

dream *verb* **dreams, dreaming, dreamed, dreamt**
1 When you dream, you seem to see things in your head when you are asleep. 2 If you dream about something, you think about it because you would like to do it.

drop *noun* **drops**
A drop of water is a very small amount of it.

drop *verb* **drops, dropping, dropped**
If you drop something, you do not hold it tightly enough and it falls out of your hands.

dry *adjective* **drier, driest**
Something that is dry is not wet or damp.

dry *verb* **dries, drying, dried**
1 To dry is to become dry. 2 To dry something is to make it dry.

Ee

each
every

edge *noun* **edges**
The edge of something is the part along the end or side of it.

eight *noun* **eights**
the number 8

elephant *noun* **elephants**
a very big grey animal with tusks and a very long nose called a trunk

energy *noun*
1 If you have energy, you feel strong and fit. 2 Energy is the power that comes from coal, electricity and gas.

enjoy *verb* **enjoys, enjoying, enjoyed**
If you enjoy something, you like doing it or watching it.

enjoyment *noun*
enjoyment is a feeling of great pleasure

even *adjective*
1 Something that is even is smooth and level. 2 Amounts that are even are equal. 3 An even number is a number that you can divide by 2.

eye *noun* **eyes**
Your eyes are the parts of your body that you use for seeing.

Ff

fair *adjective* **fairer, fairest**
1 Something that is fair treats everyone in the same way so that everyone is equal. 2 Fair hair is light in colour.

fair *noun* **fairs**
a place with a lot of rides and stalls, where you can go to enjoy yourself by going on the rides and trying to win things at the stalls

fairy *noun* **fairies**
In stories, fairies are tiny people who have wings and can do magic.

family *noun* **families**
Your family is all the people who are related to you, for example your parents, brothers and sisters, aunts and uncles.

fancy *adjective* **fancier, fanciest**
1 decorated 2 not plain

fancy *verb* **fancies, fancying, fancied**
to fancy something is to want or like it

farmyard *noun* **farmyards**
the open area surrounded by farm buildings

fast *adjective* **faster, fastest**
1 Something that is fast moves quickly.
2 If a clock or watch is fast, it shows a time that is later than the right time.

fat *adjective* **fatter, fattest**
A person or animal that is fat has a very thick, round body.

father *noun* **fathers**
Your father is your male parent.

February *noun*
the second month of the year

fetch *verb* **fetches, fetching, fetched**
When you fetch something, you go and get it.

fiction *noun*
books and stories that are made up, not true

field *noun* **fields**
a piece of ground with crops or grass growing on it

fill *verb* **fills, filling, filled**
1 When you fill something, you put so much in it that it is full. 2 If food fills you up, it makes you feel full.

find *verb* **finds, finding, found**
When you find something, you see it.

finish *verb* **finishes, finishing, finished**
When you finish, you come to the end of something.

first *adjective*
The first thing is the one that comes before all the others.

five *noun* **fives**
the number 5

floor *noun* **floors**
1 The floor in a building is the part that you walk on. 2 A floor in a tall building is one of the levels in it.

fly *noun* **flies**
a small insect with wings

fly *verb* **flies, flying, flew, flown**
When something flies, it moves along through the air.

food *noun* **foods**
anything that you eat to help you grow and be healthy

foot *noun* **feet**
1 Your feet are the parts of your body that you stand on. 2 We can measure length in feet. One foot is about 30 centimetres.

football *noun*
1 a game in which two teams try to score goals by kicking a ball into a net 2 a ball that you use for playing football

forget *verb* **forgets, forgetting, forgot, forgotten**
If you forget something, you do not remember it.

fossil *noun* **fossils**
part of a dead plant or animal that has been in the ground for millions of years and has gradually turned to stone

four *noun* **fours**
the number 4

a b c d e **f** g h i j k l m n o p q r s t u v w x y z

fresh *adjective* **fresher, freshest**
1 Something that is fresh is clean and new.
2 Fresh food has been made or picked only a short time ago. 3 Fresh air is clean and cool.

Friday *noun* **Fridays**
the day after Thursday

friend *noun* **friends**
Your friends are the people you like and know well.

frisky *adjective* **friskier, friskiest**
playful or lively

fudge *noun*
a soft sweet made with milk, sugar and butter

full *adjective* **fuller, fullest**
If something is full, it has as much inside it as it can hold.

fun *noun*
When you have fun, you enjoy yourself.

funny *adjective* **funnier, funniest**
1 Something that is funny makes you laugh or smile. 2 Something that is funny is strange or surprising.

Gg

garden *noun* **gardens**
a piece of ground where people grow flowers, fruit or vegetables

gem *noun* **gems**
a precious stone or jewel

giant *noun* **giants**
a very big person, especially in stories

giraffe *noun* **giraffes**
A giraffe is a very tall African animal with a very long neck.

girl *noun* **girls**
a female child

give *verb* **gives, giving, gave, given**
If you give something to someone, you let them have it.

gnat *noun* **gnats**
a tiny fly that bites

gnaw *verb* **gnaws, gnawing, gnawed**
When an animal gnaws on something, it keeps biting it.

go *verb* **goes, going, went, gone**
1 When you go somewhere, you move or travel so that you are there. 2 If a machine is going, it is working.

goal *noun* **goals**
1 the net where you must kick or throw the ball to score a point in a game such as football or netball 2 something that you want to achieve

gold *noun*
a shiny, yellow metal that is very valuable

good *adjective* **better, best**
1 Something that is good is nice, pleasant or enjoyable. 2 Someone who is good is kind and honest. 3 When you are good, you behave well and do not do anything naughty. 4 If you are good at something, you can do it well.

grand *adjective* **grander, grandest**
Something that is grand is very big and important.

grass *noun* **grasses**
a green plant that covers the ground and is used for lawns and parks

great *adjective* **greater, greatest**
1 Something that is great is very big and impressive. 2 A great person is very clever and important. 3 Something that is great is very good.

green *adjective* **greener, greenest**
Something that is green is the colour of grass.

grey *adjective* **greyer, greyest**
Grey is the colour of the sky on a cloudy day.

grow *verb* **grows, growing, grew, grown**
1 To grow means to become bigger. 2 When you grow plants, you put them in the ground and look after them.

Hh

hair *noun* **hairs**
Your hair is the long, soft stuff that grows on your head. An animal's hair is the soft stuff that grows all over its body.

half *noun* **halves**
One half of something is one of two equal parts that the thing is divided into. It can also be written as ½.

happily *adverb*
To do something happily is to do it in a happy way.

happiness *noun*
being happy

happy *adjective* **happier, happiest**
When you are happy, you feel pleased and you are enjoying yourself.

have *verb* **has, having, had**
1 If you have something, you own it. 2 If you have an illness, you are suffering from it. 3 If you have to do something, you must do it.

head *noun* **heads**
1 Your head is the part at the top of your body that contains your brain, eyes and mouth. 2 The head is the person in charge of something.

hear *verb* **hears, hearing, heard**
When you hear something, you notice it through your ears.

here *adverb*
in this place

high *adjective* **higher, highest**
1 Something that is high is very tall. 2 Something that is high up is a long way above the ground. 3 A high voice or sound is not deep or low.

hike *noun* **hikes**
a long walk in the countryside

hike *verb* **hikes, hiking, hiked**
To hike is to go for a long walk in the countryside.

hiker *noun*
someone who goes for long walks in the countryside

hold *verb* **holds, holding, held**
1 When you hold something, you have it in your hands. 2 The amount that something holds is the amount that you can put inside it.

hole *noun* **holes**
a gap or an empty space in something

home *noun* **homes**
Your home is the place where you live.

hope *verb* **hopes, hoping, hoped**
If you hope that something will happen, you want it to happen.

hopeless *adjective*
1 You say that something is hopeless when you think that it is never going to work. 2 If you are hopeless at something, you are very bad at it.

horse *noun* **horses**
a big animal that people can ride on or use to pull carts

hospital *noun* **hospitals**
a place where people who are ill or hurt are looked after until they are better

hour *noun* **hours**
We measure time in hours. There are sixty minutes in one hour and 24 hours in one day.

house *noun* **houses**
a building where people live

how *adverb*
1 a word that you use to ask questions 2 a word that you use to explain the way something works or happens

huge *adjective*
Something that is huge is very big.

hum *verb* **hums, humming, hummed**
When you hum, you sing a tune with your lips closed.

hunt *verb* **hunts, hunting, hunted**
1 To hunt means to chase and kill animals for food or as a sport. 2 When you hunt for something, you look for it in a lot of different places.

hunter *noun* **hunters**
someone who hunts for sport

hurt *verb* **hurts, hurting, hurt**
1 To hurt someone means to make them feel pain. 2 If a part of your body hurts, it feels sore.

hutch *noun* **hutches**
a small box or cage that you keep a pet rabbit in

Ii

ice *noun*
water that has frozen hard

improve *verb* **improves, improving, improved**
1 To improve something means to make it better.
2 When something improves, it gets better.

instead *adverb*
in place of something else

Jj

jacket *noun* **jackets**
a short coat

January *noun*
the first month of the year

jar *noun* **jars**
a glass container that food is kept in

jog *verb* **jogs, jogging, jogged**
1 When you jog, you run slowly. 2 If you jog something, you knock it or bump it.

join *verb* **joins, joining, joined**
1 When you join things together, you fasten or tie them together. 2 When you join a club or group, you become a member of it.

July *noun*
the seventh month of the year

jump *verb* **jumps, jumping, jumped**
When you jump, you push yourself up into the air.

jumper *noun* **jumpers**
a warm piece of clothing with long sleeves which you wear on the top half of your body

June *noun*
the sixth month of the year

Kk

key *noun* **keys**
1 a piece of metal that is shaped so that it fits into a lock 2 The keys on a piano or computer keyboard are the parts that you press to make it work.

kind *noun* **kinds**
a type

kind *adjective* **kinder, kindest**
Someone who is kind is friendly and nice to people.

kit *noun* **kits**
1 the clothes and other things that you need to do a sport 2 a set of parts that you fit together to make something

kitchen *noun* **kitchens**
the room in a house in which people prepare and cook food

knee *noun* **knees**
Your knee is the part in the middle of your leg, where your leg can bend.

knight *noun* **knights**
a man who wore armour and rode into battle on a horse, in the past

A B C D E F G H I J K L M N O P Q R S T U V W X Y Z

knock *verb* **knocks, knocking, knocked**
When you knock something, you bang it or hit it.

know *verb* **knows, knowing, knew, known**
1 If you know something, you have learnt it and have it in your mind. 2 If you know someone, you have met them before and you recognize them.

Ll

last *adjective*
The last thing is the one that comes after all the others.

last *verb* **lasts, lasting, lasted**
If something lasts for a certain time, it goes on for that amount of time.

lie *noun* **lies**
something you say that you know is not true

lie *verb* **lies, lying, lied**
When you lie, you say something that you know is not true.

lie *verb* **lies, lying, lay, lain**
1 When you lie down, you rest with your body spread out on the ground or on a bed. 2 When something lies somewhere, it is there.

light *noun* **lights**
1 Light is brightness that comes from the sun, the stars, fires and lamps. Light helps us to see things. 2 A light is a lamp, bulb or torch that gives out light.

light *adjective* **lighter, lightest**
1 Something that is light is not heavy. 2 A place that is light is not dark, but has plenty of light in it.

light *verb* **lights, lighting, lit**
1 To light something means to put light in it so that you can see. 2 To light a fire means to make it burn.

like *verb* **likes, liking, liked**
1 If you like something, you think it is nice. If you like someone, you think that they are nice. 2 If one thing is like another, it is similar to it.

little *adjective*
1 Something that is little is not very big. 2 If you have little of something, you do not have very much.

live *verb* **lives, living, lived**
1 To live means to be alive. 2 If you live somewhere, that is where your home is.

live *adjective*
1 A live animal is alive. 2 A live television programme is not recorded, but is shown as it is happening.

love *verb* **loves, loving, loved**
1 If you love someone, you like them very much. 2 If you love something, you like it a lot.

Mm

machine *noun* **machines**
A machine has parts that work together to do a job.

magic *noun*
In stories, magic is the power that some people have to make impossible and wonderful things happen.

make *verb* **makes, making, made**
1 When you make something, you create it. 2 To make something happen means to cause it to happen. 3 If you make someone do something, you force them to do it. 4 If you make something up, you invent it and it is not true.

many
Many means a large number.

March *noun*
the third month of the year

May *noun*
the fifth month of the year

mean *verb* **means, meaning, meant**
When you say what a word means, you say what it describes or shows.

mean *adjective* **meaner, meanest**
1 Someone who is mean does not like sharing things. 2 Someone who is mean is unkind.

a b c d e f g h i j k l m n o p q r s t u v w x y z

A B C D E F G H I J K L **M** **N** O P Q R S T U V W X Y Z

meat *noun*
the flesh from animals that we can eat

meet *verb* meets, meeting, met
1 When people meet, they see each other and talk to each other. 2 When two roads or rivers meet, they join together.

merriment *noun*
a lively time, fun or enjoyment

metal *noun* metals
Metal is a strong material. Gold, silver, iron and tin are all types of metal.

metre *noun* metres
We can measure length in metres.

middle *noun*
1 the part near the centre of something, not at the edges 2 the part that is not near the beginning or end of something

millimetre *noun* millimetres
We can measure length in millimetres.

mind *noun* minds
Your mind is your ability to think and all the thoughts, ideas and memories that you have.

mind *verb* minds, minding, minded
If you do not mind about something, it does not upset or worry you.

miss *verb* misses, missing, missed
1 If you miss something, you do not catch it or hit it. 2 If you miss someone, you feel sad because they are not with you.

mix *verb* mixes, mixing, mixed
When you mix things together, you put them together and stir them.

Monday *noun* Mondays
the day after Sunday

money *noun*
the coins and pieces of paper that we use to buy things

monkey *noun* monkeys
A monkey is a furry animal with a long tail. Monkeys are very good at climbing and swinging in trees.

moon *noun*
The moon is the large, round thing that you see shining in the sky at night. The moon travels round the earth in space.

more *adjective*
a bigger number or amount

morning *noun* mornings
the time from the beginning of the day until the middle of the day

most *adjective*
more than any other

mother *noun* mothers
Your mother is your female parent.

motion *noun* motions
1 a way of moving 2 movement

mouth *noun* mouths
Your mouth is the part of your face that you can open and use for eating and speaking.

move *verb* moves, moving, moved
1 When you move something, you take it from one place and put it in another place. 2 When something moves, it goes from one place to another.

Mr *noun*
a title you put before a man's name

Mrs *noun*
a title you put before a married woman's name

much *adjective* more, most
a lot

Nn

national *adjective*
belonging to a nation or country

near *adverb*
not far away

new *adjective* **newer, newest**
1 Something that is new has just been made or bought and is not old. 2 Something that is new is different.

nice *adjective* **nicer, nicest**
1 Something that is nice is pleasant or enjoyable. 2 Someone who is nice is kind.

night *noun* **nights**
the time when it is dark

nine *noun* **nines**
the number 9

nostril *noun* **nostrils**
Your nostrils are the two holes at the end of your nose, which you breathe through.

notch *noun* **notches**
a small V-shaped cut or mark

noun *noun* **nouns**
A noun names a person or thing.

November *noun*
the eleventh month of the year

now *adverb*
at this time

Oo

October *noun*
the tenth month of the year

off *adverb*
not switched on

oil *noun*
Oil is a thick, slippery liquid. You can use some types of oil as fuel or to make machines work more smoothly. You use other types of oil in cooking.

old *adjective* **older, oldest**
1 Someone who is old has lived for a long time. 2 Something that is old was made a long time ago.

once *adverb*
1 one time 2 at one time

one *noun* **ones**
the number 1

only *adjective*
An only child is a child who has no brothers or sisters.

only *adverb*
not more than

orange *adjective*
Something that is orange is the colour you get when you mix red and yellow together.

orange *noun* **oranges**
a round, juicy fruit with a thick orange skin and sweet, juicy flesh

other
The other thing is a different thing, not this one.

out *adverb*
1 away from 2 not at home

oval *noun* **ovals**
a shape that looks like an egg

own *adjective*
Something that is your own belongs to you.

own *verb* **owns, owning, owned**
If you own something, it is yours and it belongs to you.

Pp

pair *noun* **pairs**
two things that belong together

pal *noun* **pals**
a friend

parent *noun* **parents**
Your parents are your mother and father.

park *noun* **parks**
a large space with grass and trees where people can walk or play

park *verb* **parks, parking, parked**
When you park a car, you leave it in a place until you need it again.

a
b
c
d
e
f
g
h
i
j
k
l
m
n
o
p
q
r
s
t
u
v
w
x
y
z

A
B
C
D
E
F
G
H
I
J
K
L
M
N
O
P
Q
R
S
T
U
V
W
X
Y
Z

party *noun* **parties**
a time when people get together to have fun and celebrate something

pass *verb* **passes, passing, passed**
1 When you pass something, you go past it.
2 If you pass something to someone, you pick it up and give it to them. 3 If you pass a test, you do well and are successful.

past *noun*
the time that has already gone

pat *verb* **pats, patting, patted**
When you pat something, you touch it gently with your hand.

path *noun* **paths**
a narrow road that you can walk along but not drive along

pay *verb* **pays, paying, paid**
When you pay for something, you give someone money so that you can have it.

pear *noun* **pears**
a sweet, juicy fruit that is narrow at the top and round at the bottom

pedal *noun* **pedals**
a part of a machine that you push with your foot to make it go

pencil *noun* **pencils**
something that you hold in your hand and use for writing or drawing

penniless *adjective*
1 having no money 2 very poor

people *noun*
men, women and children

person *noun* **people** or **persons**
a man, woman or child

phonics *noun*
Phonics are the different sounds that letters represent when they are written down. You can use phonics to help you learn to read by saying the sound of each letter in a word and then putting them all together to make the whole word.

pie *noun* **pies**
a type of food that has meat, vegetables or fruit in the middle and pastry on the outside

pink *adjective*
Something that is pink is very pale red.

plain *adjective* **plainer, plainest**
Something that is plain is ordinary, and not different or special.

plainness *noun*
Plainness is when a thing is plain or simple with no decoration or patterns.

plant *noun* **plants**
A plant is a living thing that grows in the soil. Trees, flowers and vegetables are all plants.

plant *verb* **plants, planting, planted**
When you plant something, you put it in the ground to grow.

play *verb* **plays, playing, played**
1 When you play, you have fun. 2 When you play an instrument, you use it to make music.

play *noun* **plays**
a story which people act so that other people can watch

playful *adjective*
1 wanting to play 2 full of fun 3 not serious

playground *noun* **playgrounds**
a place outside where children can play

plentiful *adjective*
large in amount

pocket *noun* **pockets**
a part of a piece of clothing that is like a small bag that you can keep things in

point *noun* **points**
1 a thin, sharp part on the end of something 2 a particular place or time 3 a mark that you score in a game

point *verb* **points, pointing, pointed**
When you point at something, you show it to someone by holding your finger out towards it.

pool *noun* **pools**
a small area of water

poor *adjective* **poorer, poorest**
Someone who is poor does not have very much money.

pretty *adjective* **prettier, prettiest**
1 Something that is pretty is nice to look at.
2 A pretty girl or woman has a beautiful face.

prince *noun* **princes**
the son of a king or queen

princess *noun* **princesses**
the daughter of a king or queen

prove *verb* **proves, proving, proved**
To prove that something is true means to show that it is definitely true.

pull *verb* **pulls, pulling, pulled**
When you pull something, you get hold of it and move it towards you.

purple *adjective*
Something that is purple is the colour you make by mixing red and blue together.

push *verb* **pushes, pushing, pushed**
When you push something, you use your hands to move it away from you.

put *verb* **puts, putting, put**
1 When you put something in a place, you move it so that it is there. 2 If you put something off, you decide to do it later instead of now.

pyramid *noun* **pyramids**
A pyramid is a solid shape with a square base and four triangular sides that come together in a point at the top.

Qq

quantity *noun* **quantities**
A quantity is an amount.

quarter *noun* **quarters**
One quarter of something is one of four equal parts that the thing is divided into. It can also be written as ¼.

quick *adjective* **quicker, quickest**
Something that is quick does not take very long.

quiet *adjective* **quieter, quietest**
1 If a place is quiet, there is no noise there.
2 Something that is quiet is not very loud.

quite *adverb*
1 slightly, but not very 2 completely

Rr

rabbit *noun* **rabbits**
A rabbit is a small furry animal with long ears. Rabbits live in holes in the ground and use their strong back legs to hop about.

race *verb* **races, racing, raced**
When people race, they run or swim against each other to find out who is the fastest.

race *noun* **races**
a competition in which people run or swim against each other to find out who is the fastest

rain *verb* **rains, raining, rained**
When it rains, drops of water fall from the sky.

read *verb* **reads, reading, read**
When you read words that are written down, you look at them and understand them.

realize *verb* **realizes, realizing, realized**
When you realize something, you suddenly notice it or know what it is true.
This word can also be spelt with an **s** instead of a **z**.

really *adverb*
1 very 2 If something is really true, it is true in real life.

recognize *verb* **recognizes, recognizing, recognized**
If you recognize someone, you know who they are because you have seen them before.
This word can also be spelt with an **s** instead of a **z**.

rectangle *noun* **rectangles**
a shape that looks like a long square and is also called an oblong

a b c d e f g h i j k l m n o p q r s t u v w x y z

87

A B C D E F G H I J K L M N O P Q R S T U V W X Y Z

red *adjective* **redder, reddest**
Something that is red is the colour of blood.

reply *noun* **replies**
an answer

reply *verb* **replies, replying, replied**
When you reply to someone, you answer them.

rescue *verb* **rescues, rescuing, rescued**
If you rescue someone, you save them from danger.

rich *adjective* **richer, richest**
Someone who is rich has a lot of money.

ride *verb* **rides, riding, rode, ridden**
1 When you ride on a horse or bicycle, you sit on it while it moves along. 2 When you ride in a car, bus or train, you sit in it while it moves along.

right *adjective*
1 The right side of something is the side that is opposite the left side. 2 Something that is right is correct. 3 Something that is right is fair and honest.

road *noun* **roads**
a wide path that cars, buses and lorries go along

rock *noun* **rocks**
1 A rock is a very big stone. 2 Rock is the hard, stony substance that mountains, hills and the ground are made of.

rock *verb* **rocks, rocking, rocked**
When something rocks, it moves gently backwards and forwards or from side to side.

rude *adjective* **ruder, rudest**
Someone who is rude says or does things that are not polite.

rule *noun* **rules**
something that tells you what you must and must not do

rule *verb* **rules, ruling, ruled**
The person who rules a country is in charge of it.

runner *noun* **runners**
a person or animal that runs in a race

runny *adjective* **runnier, runniest**
Something that is runny is like a liquid.

Ss

sad *adjective* **sadder, saddest**
If you feel sad, you feel unhappy.

sadness *noun*
Sadness is what you feel when you are sad.

safe *adjective* **safer, safest, safest**
1 If you are safe, you are not in any danger.
2 If something is safe, you will not get hurt if you go on it or use it.

same *adjective*
1 Things that are the same are like each other. 2 If two people share the same thing, they share one thing and do not have two different ones.

Saturday *noun* **Saturdays**
the day after Friday

saw *noun* **saws**
A saw is a tool that you use to cut wood. It has a row of sharp teeth which you push backwards and forwards over the wood to cut it.

say *verb* **says, saying, said**
When you say something, you speak.

scare *verb* **scares, scaring, scared**
If something scares you, it makes you feel frightened.

school *noun* **schools**
a place where children go to learn things

score *noun* **scores**
The score in a game is the number of points that each player or team has.

score *verb* **scores, scoring, scored**
When you score in a game, you get a point or a goal.

sea *noun* **seas**
The sea is the salty water that covers large parts of the earth.

section *noun* **sections**
one part of something

see *verb* **sees, seeing, saw, seen**
1 When you see something, you notice it with your eyes. 2 When you can see something, you can understand it.

semicircle *noun* **semicircles**
a shape that is half of a circle

September *noun*
the ninth month of the year

seven *noun* **sevens**
the number 7

share *verb* **shares, sharing, shared**
1 When you share something, you give some of it to other people. 2 When people share something, they all use it.

shiny *adjective* **shinier, shiniest**
bright or glossy

shirt *noun* **shirts**
A shirt is a piece of clothing that you wear on the top half of your body. It has buttons down the front, sleeves and a collar.

shore *noun* **shores**
the land by the edge of the sea

short *adjective* **shorter, shortest**
1 Someone who is short is not very tall. 2 Something that is short is not very long. 3 Something that is short does not last very long.

should *verb*
If you should do something, you ought to do it.

show *noun* **shows**
something that people perform for other people to watch at the theatre or on television

show *verb* **shows, showing, showed, shown**
1 When you show something to someone, you let them see it. 2 If you show someone how to do something, you do it so that they can watch you and learn how to do it. 3 If something shows, people can see it.

shy *adjective* **shyer, shyest**
Someone who is shy is a bit nervous about talking to people they do not know.

side *noun* **sides**
1 The sides of something are the parts on the left and right of it, not at the back or the front. 2 Your sides are the parts of your body on your left and right. 3 The sides of something are its edges. 4 The two sides of a piece of paper or cloth are its front and back. 5 One side in a game or fight is one group that is playing or fighting against another group.

sink *noun* **sinks**
a large bowl with taps where you can wash things

sink *verb* **sinks, sinking, sank, sunk**
1 When something sinks, it goes under water. 2 When something sinks, it goes downwards.

sister *noun* **sisters**
Your sister is a girl who has the same parents as you.

six *noun* **sixes**
the number 6

sketch *verb* **sketches, sketching, sketched**
When you sketch something, you draw it quickly and roughly.

ski *noun* **skis**
Skis are long, flat sticks that you strap to your feet and use for moving over snow.

ski *verb* **skis, skiing, skied**
When you ski, you move over snow on skis.

skin *noun* **skins**
1 Your skin is the part of you that covers all of your body. 2 The skin on a fruit or vegetable is the tough part on the outside of it.

snow *noun*
small, light flakes of frozen water that fall from the sky when it is very cold

so *adverb*
very

A B C D E F G H I J K L M N O P Q R **S** **T** U V W X Y Z

soil *noun*
the brown earth that plants grow in

son *noun* sons
Someone's son is their male child.

soon *adverb*
in a very short time

sound *noun* sounds
anything that you can hear

sound *verb* sounds, sounding, sounded
If a bell or alarm sounds, it makes a noise.

spend *verb* spends, spending, spent
1 When you spend money, you use it to pay for things. 2 When you spend time doing something, you use the time to do that thing.

sphere *noun* spheres
A sphere is a solid shape like a ball.

spring *noun* springs
1 the time of year when plants start to grow and the days get lighter 2 a piece of metal wound into rings so that it jumps back into shape after it has been pressed

square *noun* squares
a shape with four straight sides which are all the same length

squash *verb* squashes, squashing, squashed
When you squash something, you press it hard so that it becomes flat.

squash *noun*
a sweet drink made from fruit juice and sugar

squirrel *noun* squirrels
A squirrel is a small animal with a thick, bushy tail. Squirrels live in trees and eat nuts and seeds.

star *noun* stars
a shape with five or more points sticking out all around it

start *verb* starts, starting, started
1 When you start to do something, you begin to do it. 2 When something starts, it begins.

station *noun* stations
1 a place where trains and buses stop so that people can get on and off 2 a building where the police or firefighters work

stay *verb* stays, staying, stayed
1 If you stay somewhere, you remain there and do not go away. 2 If you stay in a place, you live there for a while. 3 To stay means to remain.

steak *noun* steaks
a thick slice of meat or fish

sugar *noun*
a sweet powder that you add to drinks and other foods to make them taste sweet

summer *noun* summers
the time of the year when the weather is hot and it stays light for longer in the evenings

sun *noun*
1 The sun is the star that we see shining in the sky during the day. The sun gives the earth heat and light. 2 If you are in the sun, the sun is shining on you.

Sunday *noun* Sundays
the day after Saturday

sunset *noun*
the time in the evening when the sun goes down and it becomes dark

sure *adjective*
1 If you are sure about something, you know that it is definitely true. 2 If something is sure to happen, it will definitely happen.

Tt

table *noun* tables
1 a piece of furniture with a flat top that you can put things on 2 a list of numbers or words arranged in rows or columns

take *verb* takes, taking, took, taken
1 When you take something, you get hold of it. 2 If you take something to a place, you have it with you when you go there.

3 If someone takes something, they steal it. **4** If someone takes you to a place, you go there with them. **5** If you take one number away from another, you subtract it. **6** When a rocket takes off, it goes up into space.

talk *verb* **talks, talking, talked**
When you talk, you speak to someone.

taxi *noun* **taxis**
a car with a driver which you can hire for journeys

taxi *verb* **taxies, taxiing, taxied**
An aircraft taxies when it moves slowly along the ground before taking off or after landing.

television *noun* **televisions**
a machine that picks up signals that are sent through the air and changes them into pictures and sound so that people can watch them

ten *noun* **tens**
the number 10

term *noun* **terms**
A school term is a time when you go to school and are not on holiday.

thank *verb* **thanks, thanking, thanked**
When you thank someone, you tell them that you are grateful for something they have given you or done for you.

theme *noun* **themes**
The theme of a book or film is the main idea that it is about.

thief *noun* **thieves**
someone who steals things

think *verb* **thinks, thinking, thought**
1 When you think, you have thoughts and ideas in your mind. **2** If you think that something is true, you believe that it is true, but you do not know for sure.

third *adjective*
The third thing is the one that comes after the second.

third *noun* **thirds**
One third of something is one of three equal parts that the thing is divided into. It can also be written as ⅓.

three *noun* **threes**
the number 3

throw *verb* **throws, throwing, threw, thrown**
1 When you throw something, you hold it in your hand and then push it away so that it flies through the air. **2** When you throw something away, you get rid of it because you do not want it any more.

thunder *noun*
the loud, rumbling noise that you hear after a flash of lightning in a storm

Thursday *noun* **Thursdays**
the day after Wednesday

tie *verb* **ties, tying, tied**
1 To tie something means to fasten it with a knot or a bow. **2** a strip of material that you wear round your neck, under the collar of a shirt

time *noun* **times**
1 Time is the thing that we measure in seconds, minutes, hours, days, weeks, months and years. **2** If it is time to do something, it should be done now. **3** If you do something one or two times, you do it once or twice.

tinsel *noun*
Tinsel is strips of glittering material used for decoration.

today *noun*
this day

toe *noun* **toes**
Your toes are the parts of your body on the ends of your feet.

tell *verb* **tells, telling, told**
1 When you tell someone something, you speak to them about it. **2** If you can tell the time, you can look at a clock and say what

a b c d e f g h i j k l m n o p q r s t u v w x y z

time it is. **3** To tell someone off means to speak to them angrily because they have done something wrong.

too *adverb*
1 also **2** more than you need

towel *noun* **towels**
a piece of cloth that you use for drying things

town *noun* **towns**
A town is a place where a lot of people live close to each other. A town is smaller than a city.

toy *noun* **toys**
something that children can play with

train *noun* **trains**
something that carries passengers or goods on a railway

train *verb* **trains, training, trained**
1 To train a person or animal means to teach them how to do something. **2** When you train, you practise the skills you need to do a sport.

travel *verb* **travels, travelling, travelled**
When you travel, you go from one place to another.

treasure *noun* **treasures**
gold, silver, jewels and other valuable things

tree *noun* **trees**
a tall plant that has a thick trunk, branches and leaves

triangle *noun* **triangles**
a shape with three straight edges

true *adjective* **truer, truest**
Something that is true is real and not made-up.

try *verb* **tries, trying, tried**
1 If you try to do something, you make an effort to do it. **2** If you try something, you do it or use it to see what it is like.

tube *noun* **tubes**
1 a long, thin container that you can squeeze a thick liquid out of **2** a long, round, hollow thing

Tuesday *noun* **Tuesdays**
the day after Monday

tune *noun* **tunes**
a group of musical notes which make a nice sound when they are played in order

tunnel *noun* **tunnels**
a long hole under the ground that you can walk or drive through

turn *verb* **turns, turning, turned**
1 When you turn round, you move round. **2** When you turn something, you move it round. **3** To turn means to become. **4** To turn into something means to change and become that thing.

turn *noun* **turns**
If it is your turn to do something, you are the person who should do it next.

two *noun* **twos**
the number 2

Uu

undo *verb* **undoes, undoing, undid, undone**
1 When you undo something, you open it so that it is no longer tied or fastened. **2** When you undo a change you have made on a computer, you change it back.

unfair *adjective*
If something is unfair, it is not fair or right because it treats some people badly.

unhappy *adjective* **unhappier, unhappiest**
If you are unhappy, you are sad and not happy.

unload *verb* **unloads, unloading, unloaded**
to unload a container or vehicle is to remove the things it carried

unlock *verb* **unlocks, unlocking, unlocked**
When you unlock something, you open its lock with a key.

use *verb* **uses, using, used**
1 When you use something, you do a job with it. **2** If you used to do something, you did it in the past but you do not do it now.

usual *adjective*
Something that is usual is normal and happens quite often.

Vv

valley *noun* valleys
low land between two hills

verb *noun* verbs
A verb names an action.

very *adverb*
extremely

village *noun* villages
A village is a small group of houses and other buildings in the country. A village is smaller than a town.

Ww

wait *verb* waits, waiting, waited
If you wait, you stay in a place until someone comes or until something happens.

wake *verb* wakes, waking, woke, woken
When you wake up, you stop sleeping.

walk *verb* walks, walking, walked
When you walk, you move along on your feet.

walk *noun* walks
When you go for a walk, you walk somewhere.

wander *verb* wanders, wandering, wandered
When you wander about, you walk about in no particular direction.

want *verb* wants, wanting, wanted
If you want something, you would like to have it or do it.

war *noun* wars
When there is a war, two countries fight against each other.

warm *adjective* warmer, warmest
Something that is warm is quite hot.

watch *verb* watches, watching, watched
When you watch something, you look at it.

watch *noun* watches
a small clock that you wear on your wrist

water *noun*
Water is the clear liquid that is in rivers and seas. All living things need water to live.

water *verb* waters, watering, watered
1 When you water a plant, you pour water onto it to help it to grow. 2 When your eyes water, tears come into them.

way *noun* ways
1 The way to a place is the roads or paths you follow to get there. 2 The way you do something is how you do it.

wear *verb* wears, wearing, wore, worn
1 When you wear clothes, you have them on your body. 2 When something wears out, it becomes so old that you cannot use it any more.

Wednesday *noun* Wednesdays
the day after Tuesday

week *noun* weeks
a period of seven days

well *adjective* better, best
1 If you do something well, you do it in a good or successful way. 2 If you are well, you are healthy.

wheel *noun* wheels
Wheels are the round objects that cars, buses, bicycles and trains go along on.

white *adjective* whiter, whitest
Something that is white is the colour of snow.

whole *adjective*
1 A whole thing is all of it, with nothing left out. 2 in one piece

wild *adjective* wilder, wildest
1 Wild animals and plants live or grow in a natural way and are not looked after by people. 2 Wild behaviour is rough and not calm.

a
b
c
d
e
f
g
h
i
j
k
l
m
n
o
p
q
r
s
t
u
v
w
x
y
z

will *verb* would
If you will do something, you are going to do it in the future.

win *verb* wins, winning, won
When you win a game, competition or battle, you beat the other people or teams.

winter *noun* winters
the time of the year when the weather is cold and it gets dark early in the evenings

witch *noun* witches
a woman in stories who uses magic

wood *noun* woods
1 Wood is the hard material that trees are made of. 2 A wood is an area of land where a lot of trees grow.

word *noun* words
a group of sounds or letters that mean something

work *noun*
a job that you have to do

work *verb* works, working, worked
1 When you work, you do a job or do something useful. 2 If a machine works, it does what it is meant to do. 3 When you work out the answer to a question, you find the answer.

world *noun*
The world is all the countries and people on the earth.

worm *noun* worms
a long, thin animal with no legs that lives in the soil

worth *adjective*
1 If something is worth an amount of money, you could sell it for that amount of money. 2 If something is worth doing or having, it is good or useful.

wrap *verb* wraps, wrapping, wrapped
When you wrap something, you put cloth or paper around it.

write *verb* writes, writing, wrote, written
When you write, you put letters and words onto paper so that people can read them.

wrong *adjective*
1 Something that is wrong is not right or correct. 2 Something that is wrong is bad.

Yy

yawn *verb* yawns, yawning, yawned
When you yawn, you open your mouth and breathe in deeply because you are tired.

year *noun* years
a period of twelve months or three hundred and sixty-five days

yellow *adjective*
Something that is yellow is the colour of lemons.

Zz

zoo *noun* zoos
a place where different kinds of wild animals are kept so that people can go and see them

A B C D E F G H I J K L M N O P Q R S T U V W X Y Z

Appendix for teachers and parents

National Curriculum coverage for Year 1 and Year 2

Index

Index

Answers

P12 frog, water; **P16** big, fast; **P18** sleeps; **P20** sadly; **P25** although; **P28** smells; **P31** I **was running** to school when I dropped my glove. **P32** flew; **P33** Amir **walked** to school and **met** his friend. **P38** A comma shows where you should slow down or pause. A question mark shows where someone is asking a question. Inverted commas or speech marks show where someone is speaking. A full stop shows where a sentence ends. **P42** I have a mum, a sister and a brother. I like to eat apples, seeds, grapes and nuts. **P43** I like strawberry ice cream, although I don't really like strawberries. Danny, do you want to play football? **P44** Do n**o**t, I w**i**ll; **P58** buzzing, buzzed, buzzer; **P60** happier, happiest; **P61** later, latest; **P62** **hipp/o/pot/a/mus** has five syllables; **P63** hum + **m** + ed = hum**m**ed; **P66** colour + **ful** = colour**ful**; **P68** rainbow, afternoon, weekend.